THE
ONLY
PROPER
STYLE

THE ONLY PROPER STYLE

Gothic Architecture
in America

Calder Loth

Julius Trousdale Sadler, Jr.

NEW YORK GRAPHIC SOCIETY · BOSTON

For J.D.J.S.

Library of Congress Cataloging in Publication Data
Loth, Calder, 1943–
    The only proper style.

    Bibliography: p. 172–176.
    Includes index.
    1. Gothic revival (Architecture)—United States.
2. Architecture—United States. I. Sadler, Julius
Trousdale, joint author. II. Title.
NA705.L67 1975   720'.973   75-9094
ISBN 0-8212-0693-1

First Edition

Designed by Betsy Beach

New York Graphic Society books are published by Little, Brown and Company.
Published simultaneously in Canada by Little, Brown and Company (Canada)
Limited.

Printed in the United States of America

Contents

Elm Arcade,
by Ellen Oakford, 1889, detail.
(Yale University Art Gallery)

Foreword

Like Marcus Whiffen's *American Architecture Since 1780*, this is a book for "building watchers." Unlike Whiffen's book, however, it addresses itself to that taste which epitomizes the antithesis of classic tradition, America's symbol of democracy, and turns itself to that style reflective of the moralistic fiber of our society, namely, the romanticism of the Gothic. As such, it is conceived as a guide to sharpen our building-watching eyes to the richness and variety of our American inheritance and to enliven our spirit by an increased sensitivity to our man-made environment.

Americans are living through a period of increased awareness to the quality of our surroundings. Certainly no other art form tells so clearly the story of where we've been, as a nation, than architecture. In the face of a seeming blandness of spirit over our two-hundredth birthday, an observable increasing pride in our past hints at the recognition that our Bicentennial monument is already built and indeed surrounds us in our cities and towns, asking only to be seen and understood to enrich our lives today and tomorrow. Books such as this, informal and informative, open our eyes to the values and stories which the man-made landscapes of America have to tell us. The multifarious Gothic spires of American churches proclaimed to the world by mid-nineteenth century the prideful achievement of stability and civilization in our communities and towns. Likewise, the Carpenter Gothic fantasies of that century, made feasible by the invention of the jigsaw, rendered it into vernacular expressions based on Downing's cottage *ornée* designs, carrying on the tradition of small building construction rooted in the saltboxes and cottages of an eighteenth-century past, and brought forward into the twentieth century through the bungalow form. Thus, a pastiche of nineteenth-century inventions, philosophies, forms, and tastes create the basis of a building legacy little understood until the threshold of the present. The aesthetic giants of the nineteenth century have been ignored, snubbed, and maligned in the voguish manner characteristic of all succeeding generations. A casual glance through this book will make clear the fallacy of these misconceptions and help you share that exuberantly justifiable pride of Gothick creation which William Beckford launched at Fonthill Abbey in England as the eighteenth century closed.

William J. Murtagh
President, Victorian Society in America

PROLOGUE

Norwich Cathedral, west front

MOST OF US feel that we recognize
an American Gothic building when
we see one, yet we cannot always
be sure of what is Gothic about it
or why it should even be called
so. Certainly it cannot be authentic
Gothic, for that belongs to the
Middle Ages, an era drawing to a close when American history began. However,
certain architectural features are so closely identified with the style that when we
see them we automatically label that building Gothic, and these features are
familiar to most people whether or not they know the technical names for them.

At the top of the list is the pointed arch, from which springs the whole system
of Gothic architecture and engineering. This single innovation enabled Medieval
church builders to avoid the heavy Romanesque construction of the preceding
period, and to form a masonry system based on slender structural elements
supported by a balance of thrust and counterthrust. The aspiring shape of the arch
has in itself acquired a connotation of spiritual uplift. Second only to the pointed
arch is the buttress, the vertical mass of masonry placed against the outward face
of a wall to support it against the thrust of a vault or roof. Walls of true Gothic
buildings were made thin to convey a feeling of lightness and allow for large
windows, and buttresses were needed to hold them up. Other identifying Gothic
features are chiefly decorative in purpose—finials, crockets, cusps, foils, vergeboards, crenelations, and the rest. When enough of these features appear on a
building to give it a certain character, we call it Gothic; this in essence has been
the criterion applied in selecting the examples which follow.

In the United States we have continued to turn to the Gothic as a design source
because its forms and motifs have variously satisfied religious, romantic,

antiquarian, intellectual, and aesthetic enthusiasms. In the absence of native models upon which to draw, the quality of our Gothic interpretations has fluctuated wildly. We have been careless of the style, and painstaking with it; some designs display the strictest scholarly accuracy, while others are caricatures of their Medieval forerunners. Nevertheless, high minded or vulgar, good or remarkably bad, the recurring evidences of this Gothic strain weave a continuing theme through our artistic heritage, a tenacious thread that has not been severed over three hundred and fifty years of architectural development.

The authors have by no means attempted to write the definitive history of American Gothic architecture. The book is rather intended as an introduction to an astonishing diversity of buildings loosely linked by a common stylistic vocabulary, with a side-glance at the decorative arts because they have their own place in the story. Moreover, its purview is limited to the United States because space does not allow adequate coverage of our neighboring American nations (where the Gothic style has flourished no less than in our own), and in the opinion of the authors token representation is no compliment.

It has not been easy to arrive at a truly illustrative sampling of the literally thousands of available Gothic examples from the seventeenth century to the present day. Certain familiar buildings are included because without them the picture would be incomplete, but a number of celebrated structures, exhaustively treated elsewhere, have been omitted to make room for others that have heretofore received small notice. Moreover, because the whole is the sum of its parts, some minor and even trivial works have been included, for a book that contained only the masterpieces would give a false impression of the development of the style. Unless otherwise noted, all these buildings still stand, but certain destroyed structures and others never realized have been introduced to fill in the picture.

Architectural historians by training and inclination place great emphasis on the most original works of a society; in doing so, they pass over more imitative productions, not viewed as landmarks in the architectural mainstream, however reflective of contemporary taste these may be. Very little American Gothic architecture can be described as a significant contribution to world architectural development. Indeed, except in its later stages, the Gothic phenomenon in this country has been more an attempt to keep abreast of English fashion than a spontaneous national development. Yet all our Gothic buildings, whatever their position on the architectural scale, are as much a part of the American scene as their more inventive coevals. Over the years, a multitude of architects and builders have turned to the Gothic as the only proper style for their envisioned aims. Should this book contribute in some small way to public appreciation of the beauty, interest, or innocent delight inherent in these works, the authors' purpose will have been achieved.

GOTHIC SURVIVAL

Stadt Huys, Nieuw Amsterdam, ca. 1653.
(Harper's New Monthly Magazine, *September 1854*)

GOTHIC SURVIVAL IS the earliest form of Gothic architecture found in the New World. The term signifies true Medieval Gothic design built a generation or more after what is generally accepted to be the close of the Middle Ages in northwestern Europe, i.e., the latter half of the fifteenth century. The creators of this belated expression of the Gothic built as they did because the only way they knew to put together and ornament a building was according to the precepts of design and construction handed down from previous generations. They were neither aping an earlier style nor trying to create an historical ambience, but continuing to build in a surviving tradition; the term Gothic would have held no meaning for them. This differentiates Survival from Gothic Revival, which was a conscious Romantic endeavor intended to arouse a particular emotional response through the evocation of an historical atmosphere. Some Survival Gothic is contemporary with or even later than certain examples of early Gothic Revival; the expressions of each style may most properly be distinguished from one another by the motives of their creators.

True Gothic architecture was virtually outmoded in western Europe when the early seventeenth-century settlement of North America began. In Italy it had been abandoned nearly two centuries before, in favor of a return to the architectural style of ancient Rome, and the Classical forms of the Italian Renaissance began to spread ineluctably over the western half of the continent in the sixteenth century. New palaces and country houses may have retained something of Medieval plans and silhouettes, but hood moldings, buttresses, and pinnacles gave way to entablatures, pilasters, and obelisks. Steeply peaked Gothic roofs were masked by Baroque curvilinear gables, or discarded in favor of hipped roofs surrounded by Classical parapets and balustrades. The pointed arch, hallmark of the Gothic, was anathema to builders in the "Italian" style, and it vanishes from Renaissance work. Most of the important Spanish buildings of the sixteenth century employ Renaissance forms, and the major French palaces and chateaus of the period are clothed in Renaissance ornamentation. By mid-century the new style made its appearance in England; a number of great Elizabethan country houses, such as Burghley (ca. 1585) and Wollaton Hall (1580–88), are veritable wedding cakes of Classical detailing.

Nevertheless, France and England gave up their Gothic more slowly than did Italy or Spain, where the form had always been a trifle alien. The Gothic style, indigenous to France and England, had naturally achieved its fullest flowering there, and its popularity especially persisted in the more remote districts. In England, the almshouses, guildhalls, town halls, and inns built in the Elizabethan era, although displaying a hint of Renaissance influence in their increasingly symmetrical layouts, depend almost exclusively on Gothic forms for their detailing and ornamentation. Such centers of learning as Oxford and Cambridge also remained true to the Gothic, not because of ignorance of Classical architecture, nor even on account of innate conservatism, but because of the desire to maintain a visual order in their academic complexes. Oxford has a fan-vaulted ceiling dating from as late as 1640, and Sir Christopher Wren, at the close of the seventeenth century, finished the Medieval tower of Christchurch College in Gothic. He summed up his feeling for architectural congruence when he said of his unexecuted design for Gothic towers for Westminster Abbey, "to deviate from the whole would run to a disagreeable mixture, which no Person of good taste could relish."

The original and chief patron of the Gothic style, the Roman Catholic Church, lost its architectural influence in England with the Reformation. The instability of the English Church in the sixteenth century did not encourage the erection of many religious structures; moreover, the great quantity of extant Medieval churches sufficed for the population. Only the masons and carpenters responsible for maintaining the old fabrics retained a working knowledge of the principles and practice of Gothic religious architecture.

By the early seventeenth century English architecture was in full transition, as Gothic forms were superseded by those of the Renaissance. The pure Renaissance works of Inigo Jones set the seal on the demise of the Medieval Gothic mode. In the American colonies the situation was less clear cut. The seventeenth-century English settlers were for the most part small farmers and tradesmen who brought with them the architectural conservatism characteristic of such folk. The more worldly among them may have been aware of the great Elizabethan and Jacobean country houses, but these vast and elaborate piles were meaningless in a land where survival was the primary preoccupation. The earliest buildings erected by the colonists provided basic shelter and little else, and even when conditions improved sufficiently to allow for a more permanent quality in building, the results were vernacular structures differing little in configuration from the simpler dwellings being put up in England when the first settlers departed her shores.

4

This vernacular work was built according to systems of timber-frame and masonry construction evolved in the sixteenth century. But though their forms were developed during the twilight of the Medieval period, it would be a mistake to affix a Gothic label to these New England farmhouses or the manors of Maryland and Virginia, for they bear as little relation to the High European Gothic as a modern tract house does to a Miesian corporate tower. They were basically vernacular buildings, showing neither Gothic nor Renaissance influences. Perhaps such major seventeenth-century structures as the original Harvard College (1638–42), the Boston Town-House (1652–58), Maryland's Governor's Castle (ca. 1640), or the Virginia Statehouse, Jamestown (ca. 1635), were ornamented with some Gothic details. However, not enough is yet known of these long-vanished buildings to allow assumptions about their architectural elaboration. Two well-known examples that do exhibit some degree of architectural pretension have a flavor more Baroque than Gothic. Boston's Peter Sergeant House (1676–79, now destroyed), and Bacon's Castle (ca. 1660) in Surry County, Virginia, were both given curvilinear end gables, a feature originally developed for Italian Renaissance church facades.

It should be added that Gothic architecture was foreign to the taste of most seventeenth-century Americans. New England Puritans could have had small inclination to employ a style so closely identified with the Church of Rome. Their meetinghouses were simple rectilinear halls deriving from late Medieval public buildings, with no accommodation for mystical ritual. The Catholic settlers of Maryland probably felt some affinity for the symbolic architectural tradition of their Church, but archaeological research indicates that although the chapel at St. Mary's (ca. 1635) had a cruciform plan, and a mullion brick from the structure survives, little further architectural evidence from the early days of the Catholic colony exists to confirm this notion.

The enterprising Dutch settlers of Nieuw Amsterdam were an urban lot who built solid brick townhouses and public buildings (the Stadt Huys, for example) on Manhattan and in Albany that would not have been out of place in Leiden or The Hague. For the most part, their buildings were stylistically up-to-date, reflecting the influence of the Renaissance, except for the characteristic crow-stepped gables. These gables are frequently seen on late Gothic urban structures in Germany and the Low Countries, and on minor houses and churches in England, but are not an expression of true Gothic ornamentation or engineering. Early engravings show seventeenth-century Manhattan filled with these distinctive gables, but not one remains.

Other evidence of the Gothic in seventeenth-century America is so slight that it is difficult to make any positive statements about it. Only in Virginia do enough architectural remnants survive to indicate that the Gothic had a place in the colony's architecture. St. Luke's, Jamestown Church, and Williamsburg's second Bruton Parish Church (of which only the exterior of St. Luke's survives in its

St. Luke's Church, Isle of Wight County, Virginia, 1632(?). Right, south wall buttresses

entirety) were three Anglican parish churches which, in their buttressed masonry walls, employed distinctively Gothic structural systems. The Anglican service, retaining many elements of Catholic liturgy, requires the Medieval church arrangement of nave, choir, and sanctuary; when Virginians built their first substantial churches they had only recollections of English Medieval churches to draw upon, and relied on Gothic forms because they were unaware of any other. The full sum of American Gothic Survival architecture, including the Virginia churches, remains a tiny, scattered miscellany—quirks rather than part of a pattern. Some tracery from long-destroyed New York churches, a vestigial trefoil, a cusped doorway in California—these and a handful of other fragments form the whole of our own linear contribution to the great Gothic tradition.

The venerable brick structure that was originally known as Newport Parish Church, and unofficially renamed in honor of St. Luke in 1828, is the purest expression of Gothic Survival still standing in America. Although simple in design and modest in scale, it is a priceless architectural document. The buttressed walls, lancet side windows, and traceried east window have for three centuries formed our most direct link with the architectural glories of the Middle Ages. Except in the brickwork, St. Luke's is hardly distinguishable from its diminutive ancient counterparts dotting the English countryside, but the fact that its bricks are laid in Flemish bond (alternating stretchers and headers in every course) makes for an interesting architectural dichotomy. The building looks backward for its design, but is positively avant-garde in its masonry work, for this bond did not reach England from the continent until the late sixteenth century.

St. Luke's fell into disrepair after the American Disestablishment and stood more or less ruinous throughout most of the nineteenth century. The roof and part of the crow-stepped east gable were destroyed in a severe storm in 1887. A series of repairs were begun in 1894, culminating in the thorough and meticulous restoration of 1953–57. The buttressed walls, traceried windows, and tower are original, as are one baluster of the communion rail, the pulpit sounding board, and part of the architrave of the west door. Evidences of a chancel or rood screen, rear

6

gallery, and tie-beam timber roof were discovered in the course of the last restoration, and handsomely executed reconstructions installed. The Jacobean turnings of the surviving baluster determine the character of most of the new woodwork.

There is much controversy, not always amiable, over the date of St. Luke's construction, which is unfortunate in the case of a building of such overriding importance. The traditional, earliest, and most widely accepted date, 1632, was found on an inscribed brick during the 1890s repairs, but some contend that the worn 3 is really an 8, while others suggest that the brick itself is a forgery. It is claimed that the 1632 date appeared also in the vestry book, but this record unfortunately crumbled to dust shortly after its exhumation, from the effects of having been buried since the time of the Revolution. Another opinion holds that, while the erection of such a substantial building at the earlier date (when the colony was barely recovering from the inroads of massacre and epidemic) is most unlikely, 1682 is too late to allow of such a tardy use of Gothic. This school offers a compromise date of 1662, since in that year the Virginia General Assembly required every parish to have a church "decently built." These conflicts cannot be reconciled unless irrefutable evidence is found, but there can be no denial of the building's seventeenth-century origin or of its unique architectural importance.

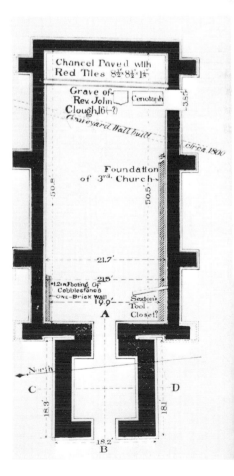

Jamestown Church, Virginia, 1644–47, plan of 1907. (Samuel H. Younge, Site of Old "James Towne" 1607–1698)

The 1901 archaeological excavations of the first brick church built in Jamestown revealed a configuration quite similar to that of St. Luke's. Slightly smaller in area, Jamestown also had buttressed walls, a south door, and a west tower. The ruin of the tower still stands. Unlike St. Luke's tower, it was built as a separate structure at least three years after the main body of the church was completed in 1644. Whether precedent of design belongs to St. Luke's or to Jamestown must remain a question until the precise date of the former is determined. In any case, the convincing Jamestown Church reconstruction, carried out by the Colonial Dames of America in celebration of the three hundredth anniversary of the founding of the colony, derives its proportions and most of its detailing from St. Luke's. This reconstruction was designed by Ralph Adams Cram (q.v.), most eminent among American Gothic Revival architects, and it is a happy circumstance that the man who gave us some of our greatest Gothic monuments should have had a hand in the renascence of this historic Gothic Survival church.

The tower, like St. Luke's, has a round arch window (the sill of which fell in long ago) above the entrance. This window may have had Gothic tracery similar to that of its sister church, but the pargeting of the jambs has made it impossible to tell. The original finish of the top is uncertain; some authorities suggest that it was crenelated, while others are of the opinion that it had a wooden belfry.

The excavation also uncovered, just in front of the chancel, another and rather surprising Medieval relic: a knight's slab tomb, originally inlaid with a brass figure of the knight and his coat of arms. The brasses disappeared long ago, but the slab

7

remains, the only known indigenous example of this ancient form of funeral art. It is now believed that the occupant of the tomb is Sir George Yeardley, an early governor of Virginia.

The second church of Bruton Parish in Williamsburg was also designed to have its brick walls buttressed in the Gothic manner, and its interior dimensions were approximately the same as St. Luke's, as shown by its foundations just north of the third and present Bruton Parish Church. A crude drawing of 1702 by a Swiss traveler, Franz Ludwig Michel, shows the building ornamented with curvilinear gable ends similar to those at Bacon's Castle, but without the buttresses. Because archaeological excavation clearly revealed the foundations of buttresses, it is thought that they may have been omitted above ground level when the original contractor, George Marable, was replaced in 1681. The church lacked a tower, although one seems to have been planned, probably as a separate structure like that of Jamestown. One Medieval feature indicated by the Michel drawing is a lychgate, or covered gateway, at the entrance to the churchyard, where, according to Medieval funeral custom, the coffin could be set down to await the arrival of the clergyman. Completed in 1685, before Williamsburg became the capitol, the building was taken down after the erection of the original portion of the present church in 1715.

Yeocomico Church is much more transitional in character than Jamestown or St. Luke's, but it incorporates several features which, although typical of the

Yeocomico Church,
Westmoreland County,
Virginia, 1706

Medieval English parish church, are found in no other colonial buildings here. The most obvious holdover is the open side porch sheltering the main entrance. Almost every Medieval church had such a porch, often used for baptisms or as a place to transact business, the location serving as a warranty of good faith. The entrance within the porch contains another Medieval echo, the only original wicket door (one set into a larger door for use in inclement weather) in the country. The chief Gothic feature of the church is the group of cement-faced panels forming a round trefoil above the porch entry, a decorative device frequently found on the doorheads of Gothic buildings.

As originally completed in 1698, the first Trinity Church in New York was a small, square structure with tall, round-arched openings divided by masonry (probably brick) mullions forming Y tracery. Whether or not the tower and its octagonal spire were part of the original design is uncertain; by 1711, however, a sum had been made up by subscription for "finishing the steeple." Early prints show the tower with Gothic windows as well as shallow corner buttresses. The church was enlarged in 1737 by increasing the length of the nave and adding the rounded apse. The apse windows, like those in the original portion, had mullions forming Gothic tracery. In 1776 the building was destroyed in the widespread fires started by demonstrators against the return of Royal troops. Portions of its walls stood in ruins until the close of hostilities, when the congregation was able to plan for a new structure on the site.

Dating from 1715, the otherwise traditional Protestant Dutch Church in Albany displayed a Gothic holdover in the Y tracery of its windows. Before the introduction of sliding wooden sashes this tracery provided the most practical method of dividing a round-arched window in order to provide sufficient support for leaded glass, and the resulting pointed half-arches gave the building an inadvertently Gothic appearance. The church was demolished in 1806.

Left, the first Trinity Church, New York, as enlarged in 1737. An 1859 lithograph. (J. Sadler Collection)

Right, Protestant Dutch Church, Albany, 1715. (American Magazine, July 1850)

San Carlos Borromeo, Carmel, California, 1793–97, sacristy door

Elements of Gothic Survival architecture are extremely rare in buildings of our formerly Spanish territories. Elaborate Gothic vaulting and other Medieval details are not uncommon in early Mexican and Central American churches, but later Spanish Colonial buildings surviving within the borders of the United States generally reflect a Renaissance or Baroque influence, if in a highly provincial form. San Carlos Borromeo Mission Church is an unusually late exception, the most ambitious and splendid church in California when it was built in the 1790s. The master mason and probable designer was Manuel Esteban Ruiz, an amateur architect who came to Carmel to instruct Indian converts in the art of masonry. The idiom of the building is primarily Spanish Renaissance, and yet a true Gothic tierceron vault is used in the baptistery ceiling and a star-and-quatrefoil window in the center of the facade. A most intriguing Gothic echo is the handsome doorway between the nave and the sacristy. Gothic clustered columns with shaft rings and bases of Gothic moldings flank the doors, and the low opening is topped by an undulating cusped and foiled arch in distinctively Spanish style.

10

THE GOTHICK TASTE

The "cabinet" at Strawberry Hill.
(The Works of Horatio Walpole, *1798*)

HAVING TAKEN IT for granted for nearly two hundred years, England rediscovered her Medieval heritage in the mid-eighteenth century. The awakening began in literature, with the Gothic mood in the work of such poets as Alexander Pope and David Mallet. Their inspiration was the disquieting romanticism of a dim Medieval past, filled with melancholy and even terror. Ruins of castles and abbeys about them evoked the temper of long ago. In *Eloise to Abelard* Pope evokes a Gothic spell: In these lone walls (their days eternal bound)/These moss-grown domes with spiry turrets crowned,/Where awful arches make a noonday night,/And dim windows shed a solemn light; . . . The inspiration of such verses, and a growing antiquarian movement, stimulated a renewed scrutiny of Medieval architecture. English gentlemen of the period began to take a dilettantish interest in old buildings, just as they did in science and the arts; the most vivid embodiment of these concerns was Strawberry Hill, the Thames-side villa of Horace Walpole. "One has a satisfaction of imprinting the gloom of abbeys and cathedrals on one's house," wrote Walpole. He did just that. Beginning in the 1750s he transformed Strawberry Hill, "a little plaything house," into a Gothic fantasy where practically all the architectural motifs of the Middle Ages were reduced to incredibly intricate interior decoration. Room after room was gothicized; chimney pieces, floors, wallpapers, and furniture reflected the Gothic taste. For the sociable Walpole, Strawberry Hill was a Gothic stage, set for what he called "the puppet show of the times," and it at once turned the Gothic into a fad among the *haut ton* of England. In this unique creation, Gothic emerged as an almost limitless source for interior decoration and exterior frills.

Strawberry Hill was both a prototype and an archetype, but throughout the century, Gothic remained but one of a number of exotic styles in which a gentleman might embellish a room, a tea nook, or a garden temple. It received particularly stiff competition from the Chinese style, and many of the architectural pattern-books of the period include suggested designs in both idioms. But China was far away; actual examples could not be observed at first hand, and the Chinese taste never developed beyond light-hearted fantasy. Gothic, on the contrary, was native to England, and authentic specimens were everywhere to be seen; their very ubiquity was conducive to a persistent and deepening interest.

The first person to treat the Gothic style in what might be termed a scholarly manner was Batty Langley (1696–1751), an architect and the author of numerous architectural pattern-books. During the 1720s and '30s he undertook a serious examination of English Medieval buildings in an attempt to discover and codify the rules which he believed to govern, like those for the Classical orders, the different manifestations of the Gothic. In 1742 he published one of the first books ever devoted to the style, *Gothic Architecture Improved by Rules and Proportions in Many Grand Designs*, in which he illustrated what he interpreted to be the Gothic "orders" and showed in a series of plans how they could be applied to contemporary works. Although he had a genuine appreciation for Medieval building, Langley evidently did not believe that the style should be used for major structures; all his plates show designs for summer houses and the like, rendered—like Walpole's exercises—in what is almost Gothic filigree.

Other English architects followed Langley with publications illustrating Gothic design. In 1752 the brothers William and John Halfpenny produced *Chinese and Gothic Architecture Properly Ornamented* in which they provided elaborate schemes for country houses in both the Chinese and Gothic styles. In the same year they published *Rural Architecture in the Gothic Taste*, showing additional examples of country houses in the style. Thomas Lightoler's *The Gentleman's and Farmer's Architect* (1762) illustrates designs for Gothic farm buildings and sham ruins calculated to add a picturesque aspect to a country property.

Many other English architectural works contained Gothic designs, but those mentioned above are known to have found their way to the American colonies, and into the possession of several builders, including William Buckland and Peter Harrison. Only a few scattered examples of the style survive from the Colonial period, however, and there is little indication that it received a great deal of attention. Most colonists were too hard pressed by immediate practical concerns to interest themselves in the architectural fads of the leisured British gentry. Those planters and merchants who did build fine houses were highly conservative in their architectural tastes, and their dwellings were rarely much more than pared-down, no-nonsense versions of the conventional Georgian houses of the mother country. In the uncommon instances where individuals were able to secure the artisans necessary to indulge in architectural elaboration, the result was generally some foliated Rococo ornaments in overmantels or ceilings, possibly a Chinese lattice railing, but practically never anything Gothic. Perhaps the New England Puritans and the Pennsylvania Quakers still felt a discomforting relationship between the Gothic style and the Catholic Church, for the few surviving examples of Colonial Gothic are mostly in the South. One of the few Colonial references to Gothic appears in an advertisement appearing in the *Virginia Gazette* for January 6, 1767, where the Williamsburg cabinetmaker, Benjamin Bucktrout, announces that he stands ready to provide "all sorts of *Chinese* and *Gothick* PALING for gardens and summer houses."

The Gothic of Walpole and the English pattern-books was mainly a system of applied decoration, interior and exterior, consisting of stylized versions of Medieval motifs. Walpole's attempts to achieve a picturesque effect at Strawberry Hill were created almost wholly in plaster or wood; structural or material veracity never entered his mind. Langley and the Halfpennys perceived Gothic as ornamentation to be tacked onto the standard Georgian rectilinear forms, using whatever materials were most expedient. Nowhere in the eighteenth century does there appear to have been any attempt to understand the genius of Medieval engineering or the interaction of Gothic ornament and structure. This eighteenth-century approach to Medieval architecture, and the particular style it produced, is hereafter called *Gothick* in this work to distinguish between it and the very different interpretations of the style that appeared in the nineteenth and twentieth centuries. The term is chosen because eighteenth-century writers commonly spelled the word with a final *k*, a practice that was dropped in the early 1800s.

A hint of the Gothick survives in the riverside porch of George Mason's Gunston Hall. Mason began the house in 1755, but its porches and striking

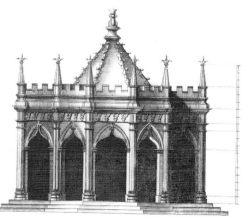

Gunston Hall, Fairfax County, Virginia, 1755–58

"An Octangular Umbrello to Terminate a View." (Langley, Gothic Architecture Improved, 1742)

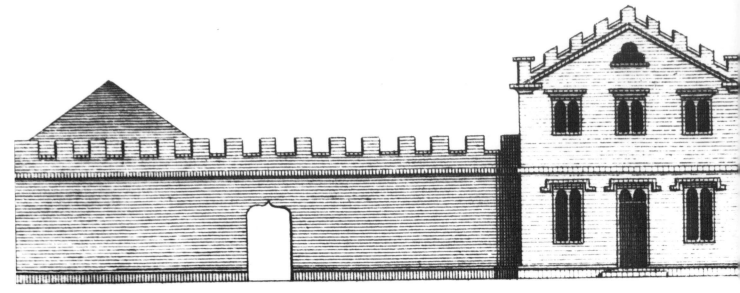

Tulip Hill, Anne Arundel County,
Maryland, ca. 1755, the Gothick hood

Miles Brewton carriage house,
Charleston, ca. 1769

14

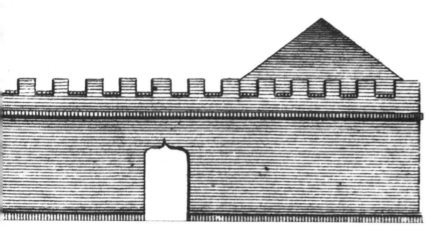

"Design for a small farmhouse." (Lightoler,
The Gentleman's and Farmer's Architect, *1762*)

interior woodwork were added slightly later by William Buckland, the English carpenter and joiner then indentured to Mason to superintend the completion of the house. Although the porch is embellished with Doric pilasters and a Doric entablature, its octagonal form and Gothic ogee arches recall Langley's "Octangular Umbrellos"; the inventory of Buckland's library, prepared after his death in 1774, lists a copy of *Gothic Architecture Improved.*

The wooden ornamentation on the hood covering the east entrance to Tulip Hill, a Georgian plantation house, is a particularly early example of transplanted Gothick. Lining the top edge of the gable are stylized crockets leading up to an equally stylized poppyhead finial. (Traditionalists claim that the finial is a representation of the flower of the tulip poplar, from which the plantation takes its name.) Entrance hoods with semidomed soffits and scrolled console supports are often seen on Stuart and early Georgian houses in England, but Tulip Hill's hood is a unique survival from the American Colonial period.

A rare example of a wholly Gothick facade is that of the carriage house of Charleston's Miles Brewton House. Although not precisely documented, this carriage house was very likely built in the late 1760s, at the same time as the main house. Its eighteenth-century provenance is reinforced by the fact that the brickwork is laid in English bond, which was rarely employed in the South after 1780. Ezra Waite, who finished the main house, was undoubtedly familiar with the currently fashionable English practice of setting off the dignified Palladian mode of a gentleman's establishment by dressing up its outbuildings as picturesque Gothick or Chinese temples; it is thus not surprising that this supremely elegant house should have been given a Gothick dependency and show Gothick traces in the forecourt wall. The facade with its triple bay, crenelated gable, and trefoil gable window, closely parallels plate 4 in *The Gentleman's and Farmer's Architect*, pictured here.

The affinity between the Gothick and the Rococo, and their common influence on Colonial decorative arts, are charmingly illustrated in the elaborately engraved trade card of Benjamin Randolph, a Philadelphia cabinetmaker. Scattered about the asymmetrically scrolled frame are various examples of Rococo furniture copied quite literally from such contemporary English pattern-books as those of Thomas

Chippendale and Thomas Johnson. The Gothick is represented by an ogee-arched window with intricate tracery, labeled "B·Rs Ware Room" (display room). Like the somewhat finicky furniture, the window, with its fancified frame, latticework, and finial composed of a mask with an eagle perched atop, displays the effusive delicacy of the Rococo. Since the window is set in a masonry wall, showing a second story, it may well be taken as an actual representation of Randolph's establishment on Chestnut Street. His affection for the Gothick is certainly evident in the chairbacks he produced in that style.

The lunette in the frontispiece of Montpelier, a mid-Georgian plantation house in Maryland, is ornamented with a pattern of intersecting ogee tracery, one of the

Labeled Benjamin Randolph side chair, ca. 1765–90. The Mabel Brady Garvan Collection, Yale University Art Gallery. The chairback is Gothick, although lacking the complex carving associated with Randolph's work.

Benjamin Randolph's trade card, ca. 1767. (Library Company of Philadelphia)

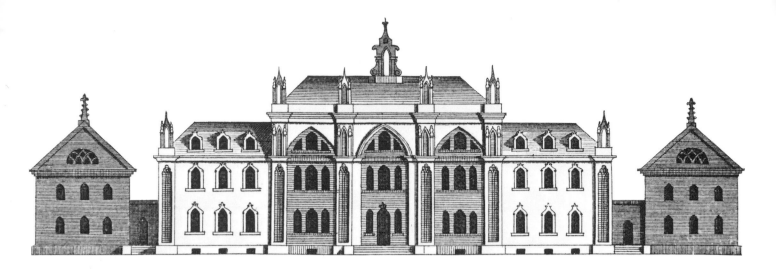

"Design for a House and Office 256 Feet in Front."
(Halfpenny, Chinese and Gothic Architecture Properly Ornamented, 1752)

Montpelier,
Prince George's County,
Maryland, 1770–71; frontispiece

most widely used Gothick motifs at the time. The tracery may be compared with the similar but less intricate tracery in the end pavilions of a country house design in *Chinese and Gothic Architecture Properly Ornamented.* Montpelier was built around 1745; the door ornament and additions were carried out in 1770–71. A similar treatment of lunette tracery may be seen in Whitehall, the villa near Annapolis designed by Buckland for Gov. Horatio Sharpe.

17

THE FEDERAL PERIOD

*"Gothic" sash design from the Philadelphia
Carpenters' Company 1786 Rule Book*

THE REVOLUTION BROUGHT few immediate changes in the fledgling nation's attitude toward the Gothic; from the 1780s to the 1820s the style was employed only in rare instances. In those cases where an architect or builder ventured to erect a Gothic building he still relied heavily on Batty Langley and the other creators of eighteenth-century pattern-books. In England, on the other hand, there was a deepening interest in Gothic. Attention was increasingly focused on native Medieval architecture, not so much as a design source for new buildings, but as a serious venture in antiquarianism. Illustrated histories of individual cathedrals (Ely and Winchester, for example) were produced, as well as general studies of specialized building types. In 1805 John Britton determined to capitalize on this highly fashionable interest, and launched a well-illustrated series in forty parts, issued quarterly, entitled *Architectural Antiquities of Great Britain*. This was completed in 1814 and followed by a series on British cathedrals which continued to come out until 1835. The question of terminology for the various stages of the English Gothic was finally settled in 1819 when Thomas Rickman's landmark publication, *Attempt to Discriminate Styles of English Architecture*, divided Gothic into three basic stylistic periods: *Early English*, ca. 1180–1250, the period of sparse, simple ornament and simple lancet arches; *Decorated*, ca. 1250–1380, the period during which naturalistic ornament and elaborate tracery was most widely used; and last, *Perpendicular*, ca. 1380–1530, characterized by thin, vertical tracery, fan vaulting, and geometric ornament. (The *Tudor* of the sixteenth century is essentially a late variation on the Perpendicular, more often associated with domestic architecture on a royal scale—Hampton Court palace, begun in 1515, for example—than with ecclesiastical works.) Rickman's nomenclature was picked up and generally adhered to in this country.

The interest of Englishmen in their Medieval heritage did not, in fact, produce any great quantity of Gothic buildings. The style remained fashionable for follies, cottages, and occasional country houses, such as William Beckford's romantic behemoth, Fonthill Abbey, but it was still considered not quite proper for important civic and commercial buildings. Moreover, few Gothic churches were built until after 1818, when the Church Building Act authorized the construction of over two hundred new houses of worship, most of which were rendered in a watered-down version of the style.

On this side of the Atlantic, the works of Britton, Rickman, and others were available, and served to satisfy a gentleman's interest in Medieval building, but they had no immediate influence on actual structures. Americans remained architecturally conservative, and new fashions were slow to gain a foothold. For most of the Federal period (1776–1830) the Gothic style was still looked upon as somewhat daring, and its rare appearances occasioned comment. The United States produced only one really major structure in the Gothic style before 1800, New York's second Trinity Church. Even minor essays in the Gothic taste, such as garden houses, outbuildings, or interiors, were rarely seen until after the turn of the century. The character of most of these post-Revolutionary efforts reflected the frilly Gothick ornamentation of Batty Langley and his followers. However, three foreign-born professional architects sought to introduce some more solid and archaeologically correct versions of the style. An Englishman, Benjamin Henry Latrobe (q.v.), was its principal advocate, but his ambitious Gothic plan for the Baltimore Cathedral was rejected, and his other Gothic works created more curiosity than demand. The French-born and -trained architects, Maximilian Godefroy and Joseph Mangin, designed one Gothic building apiece, each in a case where the particular circumstances were deemed appropriate, but neither produced any further examples. The Gothick of Langley and Halfpenny persisted, albeit in bits and pieces: in mantels, summer houses, and a very few dwellings. In Rhode Island, most notably, John Holden Greene and Russell Warren (1792–1860) made use of Batty Langley detailing on several important examples of their work dating from as late as the 1810s.

On the whole, however, buildings of the Federal period were rendered in the attenuated Neoclassicism of Robert Adam. Classical Revival forms appeared as early as 1785 with Thomas Jefferson's Neo-Roman Virginia capitol, and later in Latrobe's Neo-Greek Bank of Pennsylvania (1798). The Greek Revival superseded the Adam style in the 1820s, and dominated our architectural scene for the next twenty years; Gothic emerged only occasionally before the 1840s.

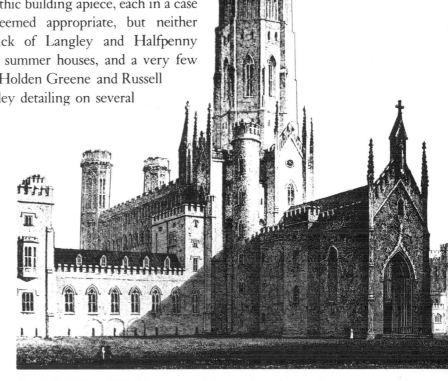

Fonthill Abbey, Wiltshire, view of the north and west fronts.
(Delineations of Fonthill and Its Abbey, *1823*)

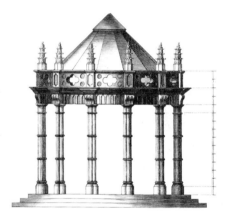

*The second Trinity Church,
New York, 1788–94.
(New York Mirror, July 14, 1827)*

*"An Umbrello for the Centre or
Intersection of Walks, in Woods,
Wilderness's etc." (Langley,
Gothic Architecture Improved)*

The second Trinity Church building was our foremost eighteenth-century essay in the Gothick taste. It stood at the head of Wall Street, on the site of the first Trinity Church, burned on the eve of the Revolution. The conscious choice of the Gothick style for a major building was extremely uncommon at that time, and was perhaps prompted by the Gothic Survival features of the preceding building. The church was designed and erected by Josiah Brady (ca. 1760–1832), who was later described as "the only architect in New York who had been a practical builder and ingenious draughtsman, writer of contracts and specifications." As is true of nearly all Gothick buildings, the church followed Medieval precedent only in its details: the body was typically Georgian, with straight-sided walls topped by entablatures and a pedimented front. For these details Brady borrowed freely from Langley, still the most popular source for Gothic motifs. The small semicircular portico follows Langley's design for "An Umbrello" with considerable fidelity. The second church stood until 1839, when, having been structurally weakened by heavy snows, it was demolished to make way for the third and present building designed by Richard Upjohn (q.v.). The drawing for the print illustrated here was made in 1827 by Alexander Jackson Davis (q.v.), who served his first apprenticeship under Josiah Brady in 1826–27.

The mantel of the Nathaniel Heyward House, which combines the Gothick with the delicate Classicism of Robert Adam, now graces the second-story drawing room of the George Everleigh House at 39 Church Street, Charleston. Its frieze is ornamented with a fox hunt, in stucco mold, framed by Gothic colonnettes and intersecting arches, as well as Classic festoons, muses, and shells. Taken from the Heyward House, East Bay Street (demolished ca. 1916), it replaces an earlier marble mantel broken in the earthquake of 1886.

Following the erection of the Miles Brewton carriage house, the English custom of supporting Georgian dwellings with outbuildings in the Gothic style gained popularity in Charleston. The William Blacklock House at 18 Bull Street is a

Mantel from the Nathaniel Heyward House, Charleston, ca. 1788

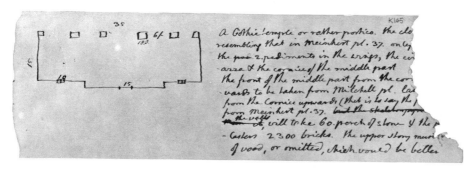

William Blacklock carriage house and garden house, Charleston, ca. 1800

Design by Jefferson for "A Gothic temple or rather portico" at Monticello, ca. 1807. (Massachusetts Historical Society)

Plate 37 from Schöne Landbaukunst

distinguished Federal townhouse built around 1800 for a London merchant. The carriage house and garden house, set well back on the large lot, are probably contemporary. Now converted into a residence, the carriage house is a simple oblong structure of two stories. Save for the original carriage door, the openings on both floors have pointed arches, the upper sashes shaped to the arch with similarly arched muntins. The garden house is almost a square, and its pyramidal roof rises to a turned wooden finial. The airy openings, with their pointed arches, are now filled in.

Thomas Jefferson (1743–1826) was one of the first and most famous Americans to be influenced by the English Romantic school of landscape gardening, which called for naturalistic parks and gardens highlighted by architectural accents. As early as 1771 he was well acquainted with this European fashion and was making plans to adorn the grounds of his newly created seat, Monticello, with temples and pavilions in various exotic and historical styles. Among his notes of that year appears a directive concerning a burial place: "In the center of it erect a small

Gothic temple of antique appearance." The temple was not built, but Jefferson retained his interest in such architectural embellishments for the next several decades. By 1807 he was seriously contemplating building his temples and started to draw plans. Among these drawings is a rough ground plan for a "Gothic temple," with notes indicating that its arcade was to be based on plate 37 of Friedrich Meinert's *Schöne Landbaukunst*, a work in Jefferson's library. (Parts of Jefferson's notes on the drawing are missing, making it difficult to determine what other portions of the temple were to follow Meinert's rather elaborate design.) Jefferson went so far as to order bricks for this project, but it is not known if any construction was carried out. In any case, the simple drawing and fragmented notes form an early and rare documentation of Gothic architecture associated with the Romantic landscape movement in this country.

The Castle is the headquarters of State in Schuylkill, the oldest social club in the English-speaking world, organized as a private institution in 1732 while its counterparts in St. James's were still public coffeehouses. The first clubhouse burned and in 1812 was replaced by the present structure, which is now on its third site. It was first shifted downstream below the new Fairmount Dam, and by 1887 the city's industrial sprawl forced its removal from the Schuylkill altogether, to a location on the west bank of the Delaware River. The move was accomplished by water, a tugboat towing a lighter on which reposed both the clubhouse and its separate kitchen. After the Second World War the building was moved to its present position two miles farther down the Delaware.

The Castle is a simple one-room building with applied Gothic decoration, perhaps inspired by such contemporary Philadelphia structures as the Masonic

*The Castle, State in Schuylkill
(on the Delaware), Pennsylvania,
1812. An 1829 engraving.
(Free Library of Philadelphia)*

The Castle

Wheelwright–Richardson garden house, Newburyport, Massachusetts, ca. 1810

Hall and John Dorsey's Gothic mansion (qq.v.). The door and window openings are rectangular, but pointed arches in black paint with tracery in white surmount them, and the eaves are decorated with scalloped, scrolled, and punched bargeboards. Throughout its peripatetic career the aim of the club has not altered; although angling no longer takes place along that stretch of the Delaware, the arts of eating, drinking, and conversation may still be, and are, assiduously cultivated. Its Citizens, Apprentices, and fortunate guests gather to cook and despatch elegant summer meals, and the famous Fish House punch is still ladled from the Export porcelain bowl made in Canton the year that the Castle was built.

The charming garden house of the Wheelright–Richardson House, since demolished to make room for an addition to the main building, was one of a number of similar ornamental pavilions erected in Newburyport in the Federal period. That garden houses in the Gothick taste should have been built in this country more than fifty years after the original publication of the English pattern-books which inspired them illustrates the protracted influence of these works. These American examples, however, were much modified versions of the elaborate English designs, and were constructed of such simple materials as board, lattice, and shingle. Their inherent flimsiness is one reason why so few survive.

The interior of the Stabler–Leadbeater Apothecary Shop in Alexandria is a rare survival of Gothick in a commercial setting. The establishment was founded in 1792, remained in operation until 1933, and is now preserved as a museum. Among the patrons who bought their remedies from its arcaded counters and cusped and foiled shelves were Robert E. Lee, Daniel Webster, Henry Clay, and John C. Calhoun. The architectural decoration of the shop delightfully illustrates the festive quality that Gothick could assume. The interior of Dr. Andrew Turnbull's similar shop of 1780 is preserved in the Charleston Museum.

24

The set of six bookcases displayed in the library of Mount Clare, Charles Carroll's 1754 mansion in Baltimore, are an important example of Gothick cabinetwork, and, considering their complicated history, a remarkable survival. Originally built around 1802 for the Philadelphia home of Dr. Casper Morris, they were removed in 1858 to Ivy Neck plantation in Maryland. That house burned in 1944, but the bookcases were spared, and were acquired by the National Society of Colonial Dames in America, which had them placed in the reconstructed library wing at Mount Clare. They appear to have been built for an octagonal room, as the four narrower cases are made trapezoidal to fit in corners, while the two wide ones have square backs and closely resemble, with their flame finials, Langley's design for a "Gothick Window for a Pavilion & C."

Horace Walpole had an admirer and emulator in James C. Johnston, of the distinguished North Carolina family. Johnston was the son of a famous politician and the great-nephew of a Royal Governor, but, like Walpole, he sought no public fame, preferring to remain a planter and pursue his literary interests. He owned a set of Walpole's *Works* (portions of which remain in the Hayes library today), where a plate of Walpole's Gothic library at Strawberry Hill is to be found. When the octagonal library was installed in a wing of his large, five-part Palladian house, it was probably more than coincidental that it was in the Gothick

Stabler–Leadbeater Apothecary Shop, Alexandria, early 19th century

Mount Clare, Baltimore, bookcase, ca. 1802

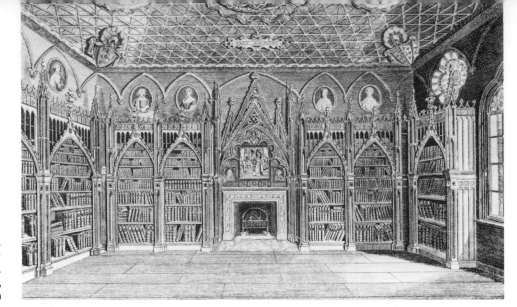

The library at Strawberry Hill. The design of the bookcases is derived from a chancel screen. (The Works of Horatio Walpole, 1798)

Hayes Plantation, Edenton, North Carolina, ca. 1818, the library

Old Georgia State Capitol,
Milledgeville, begun in 1807

taste, with details closely resembling those at Strawberry Hill. Although much less ornate, the Hayes library, like Walpole's, makes use of similar elongated panels with quatrefoils at the edges of the bookcases, and quatrefoils around the mantel; moreover, the overmantel is treated as an elaborate tabernacle for the display of portraiture. The actual design of the library may have been the work of William Nichols, an English architect at that time living in North Carolina who, Johnston family papers show, had a hand in the finishing of the house.

The old State Capitol of Georgia, portions of which date from 1807, is an unusually early Gothic public building, remarkable for that time and place. It was designed by Maj.-Gen. Jett Thomas, an officer in the state militia and a professional contractor, but stood unfinished until 1833 when the architect Joseph Lane completed the scheme by adding four wings. The use of the Gothic style for the state's most symbolic edifice is interesting evidence of advanced architectural taste. The relatively simple structure housed the Georgia Assembly from 1807 to 1868. After the legislature moved to Atlanta, the building was used as a courthouse; it later housed the Georgia Military Academy. The interior was gutted by fire in 1894, and in 1941 a blaze virtually destroyed the building. It was accurately reconstructed the following year, on the basis of drawings made for the Historic American Buildings Survey only a few years before.

The first professionally trained architect to practice in the United States provided our first mature Gothic designs. Although remembered chiefly for his introduction of the Greek Revival, Benjamin Henry Latrobe (1764–1820) is also to be credited with being our first major proponent of the Gothic. Born in England and educated at the University of Leipzig, he studied architecture in London under Samuel Pepys Cockerell and was instructed in the rational classicism which was the dominant school of his day. He retained, however, a strong Romantic bent dating from a childhood visit to the Gothic ruins of Kirkstall Abbey near Leeds. Cockerell, an advocate of the Greek Revival, had even toyed with such exotic idioms as the Hindu, and probably fostered his student's Romantic strain. Under Cockerell's auspices, Latrobe had a promising future in England, but grief at the death of his wife caused him to quit his London practice for a new life in the New World. He settled in Philadelphia, where he entered upon the most productive period of his career.

Gothic comprises only a fraction of Latrobe's oeuvre, but in a country where the style was relatively unknown, he was *sui generis*. His Gothic marked a considerable advance over Langley's and Walpole's, and is more akin to that of the English architect James Wyatt (1748–1813), who had achieved a firm grasp of the style through his renovations of British cathedrals. For Wyatt the Gothic

was more than a decorative accent; it was a medium for expressing the intensified Romantic spirit of the age. But neither Wyatt's nor Latrobe's Gothic displays the archaeological accuracy that characterized the style in later years. Their vocabulary was primarily expressed in cosmetic terms, and bore little relation to Medieval structural systems. Latrobe's apprehension of Gothic structure was, at best, vague, and his domestic and commercial buildings indiscriminately employed ecclesiastical motifs; nevertheless, his few ventures into Medievalism are creditable attempts to capture a serious and genuine Gothic flavor far beyond the contrived Gothick ornamentation of Langley's school.

Gothic works might have formed a larger share of Latrobe's output had his designs met with a little more enthusiasm. The rejection of his design for the Baltimore Cathedral in favor of his own Classical scheme no doubt discouraged him from proposing any further large-scale projects in the Gothic style. Latrobe succeeded in building only four Gothic structures during his very active career, two of which survive. They are by no means the best of his generally masterly work, but they remain a significant milestone in the history of American taste and architectural development.

His earliest Gothic experiment was Sedgeley, a house designed for William Crammond on the banks of the Schuylkill just outside Philadelphia. Erected in 1799, and destroyed by fire in the mid-nineteenth century, it is often claimed as our first *Gothic Revival* house. Like most pre-Victorian Gothic buildings, it achieved its flavor through the application of Gothic details to basic geometric forms. The house was a regular two-story rectangular mass covered by a hipped roof. At each corner were one-story pavilions connected by one-story galleries. These elements were rendered Gothic by placing pointed arches in the pavilions, dormers, and some of the second-story windows. Other windows were topped by hood moldings with dripstones, and the eaves lined with scalloped boards. Sedgeley, although of one Romantic spirit with its counterparts in the British Isles, fell short of most of them not only in scale and elaboration but in the quality of its detailing, although it might well have been more of a credit to Latrobe had he been able to exercise authority over its construction. In a letter of 1805, writing of the perils of practicing architecture in the United States, he declared: "On the erection of Mr. Crammond's house on the Schuylkill I have been disgraced both by the deformity & expense of some parts of the building, because, after giving the first general design, I had no further concern with it."

Had Latrobe's Gothic Baltimore Cathedral been built, it would have fulfilled a deep ambition for its designer, been the first Gothic cathedral since the Middle Ages, and might have advanced the revival of the Gothic for ecclesiastical use by more than a quarter of a century. When, in 1804, John Carroll, first Bishop of Baltimore, began to plan for an impressive cathedral in the diocese, Latrobe, aware that such a commission provided a splendid opportunity for establishing his reputation, offered his architectural services free, and, not surprisingly, was awarded the job. He submitted two entirely different schemes, one Gothic and

Sedgeley, Philadelphia, 1799.
(Historical Society of Pennsylvania)

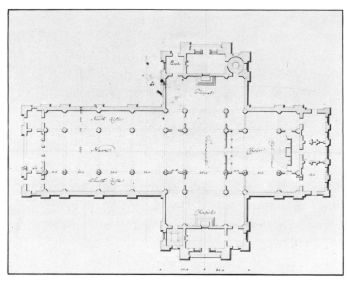

Rejected Gothic scheme for the Baltimore Cathedral, by Latrobe, 1805. Right, section; below left, west elevation; below right, plan. (Smithsonian Institution)

one Roman. Although naive in many respects, the rejected scheme was more convincingly Gothic than anything seen in this country since St. Luke's Church, and had all the features essential to an actual Medieval Gothic cathedral: cruciform plan, buttressed walls, vaulted ceiling, side aisles, and a full range of Gothic details. In general form it bore a strong resemblance to his own nostalgic watercolor of Kirkstall Abbey. The detailing might have been more polished had Latrobe not been so far removed from his sources; he complained that much of his Gothic had to be drawn from memory, as he had no models to follow. The somewhat stilted proportions and wiry details would not have satisfied him in his maturity, but at this stage of his career the opportunity to produce a full-blown Romantic creation took precedence over other considerations. In the words of his biographer, Talbot Hamlin, the design displays a "compromise between emotion and structure, between memory and imagination." His distinguished reputation was probably saved when the diocese declined the Gothic gambit and chose to build the domed Classical structure that is unquestionably his masterpiece.

Latrobe startled Philadelphia in 1800 when, in the Bank of Pennsylvania, he created the first Greek Revival building in the United States; he compounded the shock eight years later, by designing for the Bank of Philadelphia our first Gothic bank. The building was well received, however, and according to Latrobe's notes and sketches its interior must have been one of the most attractive in the city. Writing to his brother Christian in 1807, Latrobe said: "Your fondness for Gothic architecture has induced me to erect a little Gothic building in the city, the Philadelphia Bank. Externally, it will not be ugly, but internally, I mean it to be a little cabinet. The boardroom is a Gothic octagon Chapter House with one pillar in the center." According to the instructions sent by Latrobe to his pupil Robert Mills, who superintended the construction, the interior had elaborate plasterwork ceilings. A fan vault with a large central pendant, described by Latrobe as resembling a birdcage, decorated the banking room. The exterior was comparatively plain, as might be expected, and Gothic in detail rather than in form. By 1837 the bank had outgrown Latrobe's building, and like so many of his revolutionary structures, it was taken down.

St. Paul's Church in Alexandria is one of the two surviving Gothic buildings by Latrobe. Like most of his works in this style, it lacks conviction, but retains a certain appeal. Some of the flatness of the facade is relieved by the three tall arches reminiscent of the west front of Peterborough Cathedral. The building has its shortcomings, but they are due, at least in part, to departures from the architect's design. Latrobe, who did not supervise the work, was aghast when he learned of the modifications that had been made. An 1817 letter to the rector reads: "I have given you the best design which I could find on the foundations of your church . . . I now find from Mr. Bosworth that not only is the whole church lowered eighteen inches, but square windows are put in the flanks. What a confession of ostentatious poverty!" Latrobe's other remaining Gothic effort, Christ Church on Capitol Hill in Washington, D.C. (erected 1806–07) has been so altered and enlarged that its original exterior appearance is unrecognizable. From all

Left, Bank of Philadelphia, 1807–08. (Library of Congress)

Right, St. Paul's Church, Alexandria, 1817

Masonic Hall, Philadelphia, 1809–11.
(The Athenaeum of Philadelphia)

indications it was a fairly plain brick building with a minimum of ornament. Its present, somewhat homely, facade is largely the result of an 1849 remodeling.

Latrobe's gifted pupil, William Strickland (1788–1854), began his career at twenty-two with the design for Philadelphia's Masonic Hall. Rather than Greek Revival, for which he became famous, he employed the appropriately mystical Gothic style. Like Latrobe's buildings, the Masonic Hall had a rather flat exterior, its Gothic details superficially applied to basic rectilinear forms. The spire had a pleasing delicacy, however, and helped make the hall one of Philadelphia's major architectural landmarks. The building was also a prototype for scores of Gothic Masonic temples erected throughout the country in the nineteenth century. Latrobe himself thought but little of the work. Writing in 1813, he complained: "The Free Masons' Hall, which is anything but Gothic, has made me repent a thousand times that I ventured to exhibit a specimen of that architecture. My mouldings & window heads appear in horrid guise from New York to Richmond." The building burned in 1818, doubtless unmourned by Latrobe. But his mentor's harsh appraisal failed to deter Strickland from designing several other Gothic buildings, as exemplified by Grace Church, Cismont, Virginia (1847), and the remodeled exterior of Immanuel Church, New Castle, Delaware (1820–22).

32

St. Mary's Seminary Chapel,
Baltimore, 1806–08.
Left, drawing by Godefroy;
right, flying buttress.

The handsome little chapel of the former Sulpician Academy of St. Mary's
Seminary, Baltimore, is often stated to be the first Gothic Revival church erected
in this country. The claim is moot, since what is meant by the term Gothic
Revival is a matter of personal interpretation. It may be valid if Gothic Revival is
defined in its strictest sense, i.e. exclusive of Gothick. However, if the broad
definition is taken—conscious employment of the style to achieve an historical,
romantic, or picturesque effect—then the chapel's claim is antedated (by the
second Trinity Church) by nearly twenty years. In any case, its Gothic-detailed
facade, buttressed sides, and vaulted interior make it the most thoroughly and
conscientiously Gothic building seen in the United States up to that time. The
architect was Maximilian Godefroy (ca. 1765–ca. 1845), who settled in Baltimore
in 1805 and taught architectural drawing and military engineering as well as
conducting his practice. It is possible that Godefroy was encouraged to design a
Gothic building by Latrobe. From Pittsburgh in 1808, Latrobe wrote to him
enthusiastically: "I understand that it [the chapel] has at last like a butterfly
crawled out of its chrysalis into a state of exquisite beauty." The chapel still
stands, unaltered from the original scheme here shown save for the lack of a spire
and of the statues in the parapet arcade. A spire, by Robert Cary Long, Jr., was
added in 1840 but taken down in 1916. It is not known how closely it resembled

Left, Federal Street Church, Boston, 1809

Right, St. Patrick's Cathedral, Mott Street, New York, 1809–15. (New York Mirror, May 15, 1830)

Godefroy's conception. The flying buttresses represent the first use of that distinctively Gothic structural device in this country. They are placed in a rather curious manner, however, in support of the front parapet; it is as if an effort had been made to emphasize, rather than play down, the chapel's facadism.

Other than the spire of Old Kenyon (q.v.), the Federal Street Church in Boston is Charles Bulfinch's (1763–1844) only known essay in the Gothic, and was perhaps the first consciously Gothic church in New England. Built in 1809, it was pulled down in 1859 when the congregation moved to a more fashionable location on Arlington Street. Bulfinch's reason for employing the Gothic style is plainly stated in a letter from his mother to a niece in London: "My son . . . has given the proprietors a Gothic plan, wishing to introduce something new among us." She accurately noted that the church's design was particularly appropriate for its minister, the Romanticist William Ellery Channing. Bulfinch drew most of the details from his copy of Thomas Wharton's *Essays on Gothic Architecture* (1800). As this rare photograph shows, the carefully articulated steeple demonstrates how competently Bulfinch could handle a Gothic form.

St. Patrick's Cathedral, Mott Street, New York, is a major, if little-known, landmark in the history of American Gothic architecture. It was probably the largest Gothic building in the country at the time of its completion in 1815. Its architect was Joseph F. Mangin, a Frenchman of whom we know little more than that he was associated with John McComb, Jr., in the design of the famous Neoclassic New York City Hall. The massive brownstone church was burned out in 1866, when James Renwick's cathedral on Fifth Avenue had already taken over its name and function (q.v.). Rebuilt two years later, it was somewhat altered in

34

John Dorsey's mansion, Philadelphia, 1809. (Port Folio, 1811)

design, but the original walls were preserved and still stand at the corner of Mott and Prince Streets in lower Manhattan. The interior was divided by six clustered columns on each side, surmounted by Gothic arches. The columns and arches were repeated in paint on the rear wall, so that they appeared to march away behind the altar into infinity. A print after A. J. Davis's drawing of 1830 shows the exterior to have been Gothic chiefly in detail; Mangin could not completely divorce himself from the Classical influence, as the straight-sided walls, topped by an entablature and balustrade, show.

One of the few houses known to have been built in this country with a true Gothick exterior was a curious Philadelphia mansion somewhat belatedly designed and built in 1809 by John Dorsey, auctioneer, politician, and amateur architect. Although on a much smaller scale, the richly detailed house held its own with earlier English counterparts, and stood in exotic contrast to Philadelphia's monotonous rows of brick townhouses. An article of 1811 in *Port Folio* described it as a "correct and chaste specimen of the Gothic order." Of its embellishments the article noted: "The walls of the porch, and the jams [*sic*], and soffits of the entrances are enriched with antique quatrefoil guiloches, shields, escutcheons and tablets, with appropriate bass-relief sculptures in artificial stone, by the celebrated Mr. Coade." Less than two years after it was completed, the house was leased as a boarding school, and has long since disappeared.

35

John Holden Greene (1777–1850) was one of the few New England master builders to employ Gothick motifs in his work. One of his most original houses was built in Providence for Sullivan Dorr, a worldly and widely traveled merchant who was not to be intimidated by unusual architecture. In this design Greene has combined late Georgian and Gothick elements in a most effective manner. The roof of the delicate front porch has a Gothick frieze, resembling that in the portico of his nearby St. John's Cathedral, and the porch roof is supported by Gothic clustered columns with shaft rings. The frieze and columns are echoed in the ornamentation of the Palladian window, and the main cornice features intersecting Gothic arches, after plate XII of *Gothic Architecture Improved*.

"A second Gothic Entablature for Order IV." (*Langley*, Gothic Architecture Improved)

Sullivan Dorr House, Providence, 1809

St. John's Cathedral is Greene's finest and most complete Gothick essay. Although he later made use of intersecting and Y tracery in the windows of the First Unitarian Church of Providence (1816), and in the Independent Presbyterian Church of Savannah (1817–19), these prodigious churches are more in the Neoclassic style of James Gibbs. In St. John's, the stiff, attenuated detailing is entirely in Batty Langley Gothick and the semicircular portico closely follows Langley's designs for garden temples. The structure is basically a standard Federal form onto which the pattern-book detailing is tacked, but Greene does show genuine originality in his self-assured handling of space and ornament in the vaulted narthex. The building was enlarged in 1868, and again in 1905, so that of the original interior only the domed nave and Gothic organ loft survive. A chapel in the Gothic style, designed by Richard Upjohn (q.v.), was added to the rear of the Cathedral in 1855.

St. John's Cathedral, Providence, 1810–11. Left, west portico; right, narthex.

Left, Linden Place, Bristol, Rhode Island, 1810, octagonal wing

Right, Bristol County Courthouse, Rhode Island, 1816

A particularly cunning example of Rhode Island's persistent Gothick is the octagonal wing of Linden Place, the DeWolfe-Colt house designed and built by Russell Warren in 1810. The main house has a somewhat complicated Classical facade, but the wing demonstrates Warren's ability to deal with Gothick motifs in a graceful and unified fashion. It is characterized by arcaded bays filled in with tall Gothic windows with intersecting tracery. The Bristol County Courthouse, only a few blocks from Linden Place, also combines Classical and Gothick details; it is attributed to Warren. The slender clustered columns of its porch are of iron.

In contrast to these Rhode Island buildings, Trinity Church (1814–16), on the New Haven Green, was a harbinger of the many Gothic structures of a more scholarly Medievalism that were to grace our towns and cities by mid-century. It was the maiden Gothic work of Ithiel Town (1784–1844), a highly influential figure in architecture during the early years of the Republic, and best remembered as the senior in the famous partnership with A. J. Davis, formed in 1829. Town studied architecture under Asher Benjamin, and settled in New Haven in 1812, where he assisted in supervising the construction of the Congregational or Center Church (shown here to the left of Trinity Church), designed by Benjamin in the elaborate Georgian style of James Gibbs. Town received much notice for this work, and on the basis of his expertise was commissioned to design the new Trinity Episcopal Church, which was to stand next door. He boldly determined to make the new church Gothic, choosing the style "as being in some respects

more appropriate, and better suited to the solemn purposes of religious worship."
Perhaps his decision was prompted by the success of Greene's St. John's
Cathedral, which had also echoed the growing popularity of the Gothic style
(albeit in an old-fashioned vein) in Church of England examples. Town's more
sophisticated detailing reflected his familiarity with Medieval churches, which he
had painstakingly studied in books and engravings.

Trinity was quickly recognized as a revolutionary work. Dr. Timothy Dwight
wrote of it: "The Episcopal Church is a Gothic building, the only correct
specimen it is believed in the United States." Apparently strongly moved by the
contrast between Trinity and its neighbors, a later writer exclaimed: "There is
scarce a more beautiful place of worship, take it all in all, in the whole of
Christendom." While perhaps not fully deserving the superlative claim, it was
certainly the most distinctly Gothic church yet seen in this country. With its
neighbors on the Green, including Town's 1827–29 Greek Revival capitol, which
has now vanished, it formed part of a remarkable architectural assemblage. Trinity
Church today is a considerably altered and remodeled version of the building
Town erected. The crenelated parapets were removed from the gables in 1844
and from the sides after 1865. The wooden upper portion of the tower was
replaced by a modified version in stone in 1870, and an apse was added to the rear
in 1885. Through a series of alterations, the interior has been almost wholly
rebuilt, and Town would recognize little more than the piers (now in stone) and
the plaster vaulting, which, although completely renewed, is faithful to his design.

*The Green, New Haven.
An 1839 engraving. Left to right,
Connecticut State Capitol,
Center Church, Trinity Church.
(J. Sadler Collection)*

39

Columbia College, New York, unexecuted scheme by James Renwick, Sr., 1813. (Avery Architectural Library)

The earliest known American design for a Gothic collegiate complex was never built. The precocious scheme is the only architectural exercise attributable to the engineer James Renwick, Sr. (1792–1863), father of the famous architect, and was proposed to alleviate the growing pains afflicting Columbia College in the early years of the century. The suggested expansion included a three-building complex inspired by the Oxford and Cambridge collegiate buildings of the Tudor period. The focal point was a library, loosely based on King's College Chapel, Cambridge, perhaps in acknowledgment of the name Columbia College originally bore. The library was to be connected by crenelated screens to flanking Gothic buildings containing dormitories, lecture rooms, studies, and kitchens. The scheme is significant not only in that it marks the first effort to impose the Gothic style on academe in the United States, but adheres more strictly to Gothic example than any previous works here, including those of Latrobe and Town.

40

Old Kenyon is probably the last Gothick structure to have been built in this country, our first major Gothic collegiate building, and one of the first important examples of the style in the Midwest. Kenyon's founder, Bishop Philander Chase, fell in love with Gothic architecture on a trip to England in 1823. Upon his return, faced with the necessity of constructing a building to house his college, he decided to consult the "best architects" regarding the plan of the edifice. In the 1820s there were still few American architects versed in the Gothic; it was by happy chance that on a trip to Philadelphia in 1826 the bishop became acquainted with the Rev. Norman Nash, an amateur architect with leanings toward the Gothic. Nash was commissioned to plan the building, and very shortly he produced drawings for a large H-shaped structure of Gothick character not unlike that of the much earlier Miles Brewton carriage house. This old-fashioned Gothick look probably derived from Nash's reliance on eighteenth-century pattern-books, available to him in Philadelphia libraries.

In 1828 Bishop Chase visited Washington and chanced to meet Bulfinch, who then held the position of Architect of the Capitol and was at the height of his fame. Chase showed him the drawings for his college and requested his comments. Bulfinch, apparently displeased with Nash's slightly squat central spire, provided the bishop with a sketch for a revised design, showing the spire much more slender and on a higher base. It was duly and accurately erected in 1829, when the central section of the building was completed. The wings, somewhat truncated, were added in 1834–36. Old Kenyon burned in 1949, but was immediately rebuilt, using many of the original stones.

Old Kenyon, Kenyon College, Gambier, Ohio, 1827–29

Sir Walter Scott.
After a painting by Sir Francis Grant,
National Portrait Gallery, Edinburgh.

THE HERALD OF ROMANCE

THE GREAT SCOTTISH novelist and poet Sir Walter Scott (1771–1832) had a stronger influence on the American architectural taste of the second quarter of the nineteenth century than any architect, native or foreign. The Gothic had a false start with Latrobe, but generally received little attention during most of the Federal period; the public simply did not display enough interest in the style to make it worthwhile for an architect to specialize in it. The many books on Medieval buildings flowing from England at the beginning of the century provided sound information on Gothic design, but served more to nourish antiquarian appetites than to influence public taste. It was Scott who virtually created the enthusiasm for the Gothic which dominated the architectural scene, as never before or since, through the middle years of the nineteenth century.

Scott's Romantic novels, with their vivid historical narrative, heroic characters, and detailed descriptions of Gothic buildings, electrified American imaginations and opened American eyes to Medieval pageantry and color. His tales of chivalry and valor dispelled the aura of mystery, gloom, and superstition that had hung about the Middle Ages, and brought the era sharply and immediately alive. The sense of drama and reality with which he imbued the period created an image wholly at variance with that established by earlier Gothic novelists·and poets. His prolific talent, and the rise of the cheap edition, combined to make him perhaps the most widely read author in America. The middle class of the sprawling young country was soon introduced to a lost epoch that satisfied its romantic aspirations.

The rapid changes brought about in American life in the 1820s and '30s by industrialization, urban growth, and technological advances had an overwhelming effect on the national psyche. The new republic came to yearn for a stability of history and tradition that seemed somehow lacking. Alienated from the mother country by the Revolution and the War of 1812, Americans were seeking elsewhere for an historical identity. Ancient Greece and Republican Rome were

42

adopted as spiritual ancestors, and the emphasis on the classics in education contributed to directing architectural taste to the temples of antiquity. Scott, however, harking back to a more innocent, if highly idealized, English age, revived a spiritual affinity for Medieval Britain. The heroes and buildings of the noble Christian era which he portrayed became the common heritage of all English-speaking peoples.

Scott influenced American taste not only through his writings but in his life style. His famous house, Abbotsford, which between 1811 and 1824 grew, under his supervision, from a small farmhouse into a baronial castle, greatly stimulated the fashion for living in a Romantic setting permeated with a sense of history. Abbotsford was no mere Gothick fantasy. It was a sprawling, irregularly massed pile, a suitable seat for a laird, picturesquely situated on the banks of the Tweed three miles above the haunting ruins of Melrose Abbey. Scott wrote: "In truth it does not brook description any more than it is amenable to the ordinary rules of architecture—it is as Coleridge says 'A thing to dream of not to tell.' "

He carried his Romantic inclinations into the interiors of Abbotsford, and in so doing started the vogue for collecting indigenous antiques. The house was filled with ancient furniture, architectural fragments, weapons, armor, and other curiosities from an earlier time, all carefully selected for their historical associations and judiciously placed to give the rooms a venerable aspect. Perhaps only Walpole's Strawberry Hill or Jefferson's Monticello had been so personal an expression of its creator. The house became a place of pilgrimage, and its architecture and contents, to say nothing of its famed occupant, made a deep impression on visitors. Among the callers was Washington Irving, who later transformed his own Sunnyside into a picturesque early Dutch manor house with crow-stepped gables and Gothic trim. Abbotsford became widely known in America. Descriptions of it greatly contributed to dissatisfaction with the chaste Greek Revival and created a longing for the evocative charms of the Gothic. This demand was met by such architects as A. J. Davis and Minard Lafever (q.v.), who unhesitatingly switched the style of much of their output from Greek to Gothic as

clients began to demand Tudor towers rather than porticoed temples, and by scores of carpenters and masons, who in the 1830s and '40s spread their naive and delightful interpretations of the Gothic style across America.

Following Scott's example, James Fenimore Cooper established himself in a Gothic setting. Upon returning in 1833 from his extensive European travels (during which he had seen Abbotsford), he found Otsego Hall, the family home

Otsego Hall, Cooperstown, New York, 1796–99, as remodeled in 1834. A contemporary watercolor. (New York State Historical Association)

in Cooperstown, standing vacant and forlorn. Inspired by the wealth of Gothic (and perhaps Gothic Revival) architecture he had seen abroad, he undertook to remodel the plain Federal house into a picturesque country seat in the English Gothic style. The plans for the remodeling were provided by Cooper's friend, the artist and inventor Samuel F. B. Morse. Morse gave Otsego Hall a Gothic porch chamber, Gothic windows with hood moldings, and battlements which, by collecting snow behind them, caused frequent leaks. The extent of Cooper's satisfaction with the remodeling is uncertain. He commented, "The Hall is composite enough, Heaven knows, being a mongrel of the Grecian and Gothic orders: my hall, however, is the admiration of all the mountaineers—nearly fifty feet long, twenty-four wide, and fifteen feet high. I have raised the ceiling three feet, and regret it had not been ten." Cooper's *Home As Found* is a fictional account of the transformation of Otsego Hall. The fascinating house was lost from the ranks of literary and architectural shrines when it burned in 1853.

The Romantic spirit touched off by Scott even allowed for such productions as the forbidding Medieval walls of Philadelphia's Eastern State Penitentiary. Designed by the British-born architect John Haviland (1792–1852), it was one of our earliest castellated buildings and a landmark in penal architecture. The prison's Bastille-like exterior belies the humanitarian concept behind its internal arrangements. In plan it consists of a central rotunda from which the cell blocks radiate in spokes to allow for better lighting, ventilation, and monitoring. Haviland's penitentiary was, at the time, an architectural expression of prison reform, and its Medieval cast was the inspiration for at least the outer aspect of countless prisons and jails erected in the country over the next century. No longer a prison, it stands empty; several Philadelphia civic groups are considering it for headquarters.

AN ARCHITECTURAL COMPOSER

A. J. DAVIS
by George Freeman, 1852.
(Avery Architectural Library)

THE INCREASING POPULARITY of the Gothic style in the 1820s and '30s made the famous partnership of Ithiel Town and A. J. Davis the leading architectural firm for residential Gothic in this country. The fame achieved through such notable Greek Revival works as the Connecticut State Capitol in New Haven and the Customs House in New York did not prevent the partnership from keeping its business booming by climbing on the Gothic bandwagon. Although Town had launched his career with a Gothic design in 1814, the firm of Town and Davis produced no significant Gothic works until 1832 when Davis accepted the commission to design a Gothic house for Glenellen, the Robert Gilmore estate outside Baltimore. The resulting villa, with its irregular massing, crenelated towers, and traceried windows, is regarded as our first fully developed example of Gothic Revival domestic architecture, and was a prototype for the many Gothic villas built across the country during the next thirty years. Davis himself confidently asserted that in Glenellen the partnership introduced to Americans the "first English Perpendicular Gothic Villa with Barge Boards, Bracketts, Oriels, Tracery in windows, etc."

As its name implies, Glenellen was inspired by Abbotsford, which Gilmore had lately visited, although the house was more Tudor than Scottish Baronial in aspect. It was demolished in 1929 to make way for a reservoir, but Davis's drawings indicate that it had elegantly appointed interiors with marble floors, vaulted ceilings, and stained-glass windows. The setting was superb; broad sloping lawns, landscaped with trees clustered in the English Picturesque manner, fell away from the terrace on which the house stood. The estate even boasted a gatehouse in the

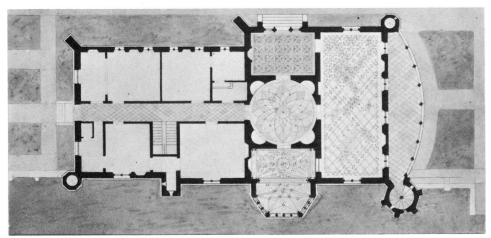

*Glenellen, Baltimore,
elevation and plan by Davis, 1832.
(Metropolitan Museum of Art,
Harris Brisbane Dick Fund, 1924)*

form of a Gothic ruin, one of the few known examples of this hallmark of Picturesque landscaping in the country.

After Glenellen, Davis went on to produce designs for scores of Gothic buildings including villas, cottages, townhouses, commercial buildings, and schools. Oddly enough, he designed only an occasional church. Although he continued to work in the Greek Revival and eventually the Tuscan or Italian Villa style, with its square towers, round-arch windows, and bracketed cornices, he is principally remembered as our foremost residential Gothic architect. Such distinctive works as the "Pointed Cottage" of William J. Rotch in New Bedford, Massachusetts (1846), or the great Gothic mansion Lyndhurst, in Tarrytown, New York, as enlarged for George Merritt in 1866, will always be cited as peaks of American Gothic Revival design. Davis's work spawned many imitators but few of them created buildings so gracefully balanced, so suavely detailed, or of such fresh inspiration.

Davis (1803–92) was born in New York City of cultivated parents. His father, Cornelius Davis, was a theologian and publisher who hoped that his son would follow a similar course. But Davis preferred drawing to scholarship and aspired to be an artist. To put such notions out of the boy's head the senior Davis sent his sixteen-year-old son to Alexandria, Virginia, to work as a typesetter for an older brother. These paternal efforts failed, for Davis returned to New York at the age of twenty with his desire to pursue an artistic career unquenched. Professional

46

artists advised him, however, that architecture was a more promising field, so Davis became apprenticed to Josiah Brady, designer of the Gothick (second) Trinity Church in New York. From Brady, Davis learned the fundamentals of his profession and probably something of the fundamentals of Gothic design as well. He left Brady after a year to open his own office in New York as a draftsman, or "architectural composer" as he preferred to call himself. During this period he put his drafting talents to work and produced illustrations of New York public buildings, including Trinity Church and the first St. Patrick's Cathedral, for the *New York Mirror* and other publications.

Davis's activities soon attracted the notice of Ithiel Town, and in 1829 the distinguished architect and inventor invited the up-and-coming designer to form a partnership. They set up an office in the Merchants' Exchange into which Town moved his famous architectural library. Through association with Town and his collection of books and engravings, Davis was able to broaden his knowledge of Gothic design. But Town's preference for the Greek Revival kept that the style for the major portion of the firm's output. The partnership lasted until 1835 and was briefly revived in 1842–43, but Davis's interest increasingly turned toward the Gothic and Tuscan modes, and after Town's death in 1844 he virtually set Greek forms aside to concentrate on those Romantic styles.

Davis continued to design Gothic buildings until he retired from practice in 1874. His later works, however, little reflect the new approaches to the style that sprang up in the years after his partner's death. Because he rarely designed a church it is understandable that he was not particularly influenced by the teachings of Pugin and the Ecclesiologists (qq.v.), with their emphasis on archaeological accuracy. It is even more intriguing that Davis was apparently not the least bit affected by the extremely popular writings of John Ruskin (q.v.), who preached the virtues of Italian Gothic forms and condemned imitation materials. Davis stuck to his stuccoed Tudor Gothic villas, crenelated parapets, sawn bargeboards, and plaster vaults. To him, Gothic remained only a means to an end, a tool for imposing a Picturesque or antique aspect on an otherwise comfortable modern home; it was hardly the philosophical exercise or expression of religious idealism that it was for the Ecclesiologists or Ruskinians.

Failure to embrace the new attitudes did not mean that Davis's work remained static. One of the last designs of his career was also one of the most forward looking. As late as the early 1870s he was working on plans for a six-story office block to be built on lower Broadway. His design anticipated modern modular glass facades by the introduction of full-height Gothic masonry piers between horizontal divisions of ornamented sheet metal. These thin members, in turn, framed what were practically floor-to-ceiling windows. Here again Gothic was a means to an end, but no less valid for that. The vertical emphasis, structural lightness, and large glass areas permeated the design with a Gothic spirit as true as that of all the weighty masonry of the Ruskin school.

Davis and his partners produced a fine design in the Greek Revival style, at the height of its popularity, for New York University, but it was, surprisingly enough, set aside by university officials in favor of the firm's proposal in Perpendicular Gothic. The Washington Square building (1833–37) was not technically the first Gothic-style collegiate building of the period, but it was certainly the most conspicuous and the most important. Much of the credit for its design must go to James Harrison Dakin (1806–52), who was apprenticed to the firm of Town and Davis in 1829 and became a full partner in 1832. He resigned abruptly in the following year, having completed his work on the university plans, and in 1835 moved to New Orleans, where he opened an office with his brother Charles and soon became one of the city's leading architects.

The great Gothic chapel of the N.Y.U. building was not included in the original plan but was later worked in at the insistence of Chancellor James M. Matthews. His visions of grandeur included a picture of himself preaching in a space worthy of his rhetoric, but when the trustees discovered that he had quietly diverted part of the school's book funds into building funds, his term was cut short before that ambition could be realized. Regardless of how it came to be built, this was one of the noblest Gothic spaces produced by the talented firm. Its great pendants and stellar vaulting recalled the ceiling of the Chapel Royal at Hampton Court, of which Town owned an engraving. The exterior was faced with Sing Sing marble and enriched with remarkable carving, and the window overlooking Washington Square was claimed to be the first major example of stone tracery in the country. It set the Gothic fashion for institutions of higher learning, a fashion that outlasted the building, which was demolished in 1911.

New York University, New York, 1833–37. Left, elevation from Town, Davis, and Dakin; right, chapel. (New-York Historical Society; Frank Leslie's Illustrated Newspaper, March 29, 1856)

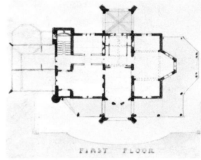

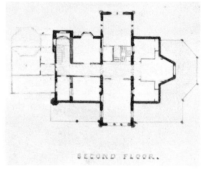

Davis designed the core of what eventually evolved into the epitome of the Gothic Revival, a country villa "in the pointed style" for Gen. William Paulding, a former New York mayor, as a summer retreat. It was erected on the east bank of the Hudson River, looking down over its rolling lawns across the Tappan Zee. A. J. Downing (q.v.), writing to Davis in 1840, commented: "I went to Tarrytown last Monday . . . Mr. Paulding's mansion I was exceedingly pleased with. I think it does you great credit—indeed I have never seen anything to equal it, as I conceive it will be when finished." Downing was so impressed with the house that he included Davis's engraving of it in his *Theory and Practice of Landscape Gardening.*

The house was constructed of gray-white Sing Sing marble, in a style afterward immortalized as Hudson River Gothic. Davis also designed appropriate furniture in the Gothic taste to carry out the mood of the house. The principal room was the second-floor library. Overlooking the river through the "Great West Window," it was lined with Gothic bookcases. It is thought that some of the side chairs still to be seen in the room were designed for it by Davis, and he further designed some additional tables for the house in 1847. In 1864 the manor was purchased from the Paulding family by George Merritt, who called in Davis once again to enlarge and remodel the house; it was eventually doubled in size and given a conspicuous square tower. Merritt rechristened the estate Lyndhurst, and added the first of its gothicized greenhouses. Under the will of the late Duchesse de Talleyrand, the property has passed into the hands of the National Trust for Historic Preservation, and is open to the public.

Paulding Manor (later Lyndhurst), Tarrytown, New York, west elevation and plans by Davis, 1838. (Metropolitan Museum of Art, Harris Brisbane Dick Fund, 1924)

49

Design for a public pump shelter,
by Jacob Small, 1818.
(The Peale Museum, Baltimore)

UNEASY TRUCES

SCOTT'S NOVELS GAVE Romanticism a firm grip on the American imagination. But though the way was cleared for popular acceptance of the Gothic, only a few individuals like Town and Davis had a real grasp of the style. This did not inhibit the erection of Gothic structures, but the buildings of the 1820s and '30s are largely marked by a casual attitude toward accurate historicism. Moreover, the Greek Revival, still in its ascendancy, gave the Gothic stiff competition. A battle of styles resulted, and some interesting compromises resulted therefrom. Like the "Colonial bi-level ranchers" of today, these naive but often delightful architectural pastiches were usually the creations of venturesome contractors rather than trained architects. Many master builders hesitated to make a full switch from Greek to Gothic because the timber framing systems they were trained to use had been developed to accommodate Classical rather than Medieval styles. Moreover, their shaping planes were made to produce moldings with Greek or Roman profiles rather than Gothic ones. Thus, if clients demanded Gothic, about all the carpenter could do was change the shape of his arches from round or flat to pointed, and add a little superficial Gothic ornamentation.

The large Nantucket Congregational Church is an excellent illustration of the conflict between Carpenters Classic and Carpenters Gothic (q.v.). Built by a Bostonian, one Mr. Waldron, its Gothic touches are offset by a pedimented facade and Classic entablature. With only a few exceptions, frame buildings of the 1830s, especially churches, remained basically Classical even though a glimmer of Gothic was peeping through the windows.

Mormon temples and tabernacles traditionally borrow from various architectural styles and blend them into an harmonious, if sometimes exotic, whole. The Kirtland Temple in Ohio combines Federal and Gothic details on a temple-form body, and may well have set a standard for the many imaginative temples that followed. It was designed by its master builder, Joseph Bump, whose workmen

Left, First Congregational Church,
Nantucket, 1834

Below left, Kirtland Temple,
Kirtland, Ohio, 1833–36

Below, St. Peter's Church, Port Royal, Virginia,
1835–36. "The ecclesiastical architecture in our
country is in a very unsettled, ill-defined state."
— Henry Russell Cleveland, 1836

form a catalogue of Mormon worthies. Joseph Smith, Jr., served as foreman of both construction and stone quarrying; Sidney Rigdon, the famous orator, was a mason; and Brigham Young worked as plasterer and glazier. The latter's skill in this regard is evident in the delicate intersecting tracery of the temple's many lancet windows.

The Washington Tomb at Mount Vernon likewise shows evidence of stylistic ambivalence. By the time of George Washington's death in 1799, the 1752 family tomb was in a deplorable state of dilapidation, and although his casket was originally placed in the old vault, where it remained for more than thirty years, he had left explicit instructions in his will for the construction of a new vault. It was not, however, until 1831, when the old tomb was rifled and a skull—erroneously taken for that of the first president—removed, that the singularly dilatory surviving executor, his nephew Lawrence Lewis, had the present vault built and the family remains transferred to it. In 1835 Lewis commissioned William Yeaton, an Alexandria contractor, to design and put up a walled enclosure for the vault. This contemporary engraving shows the pointed-arch entrance supported by its relatively Classical brick piers. The simple brick wall and Gothic gateway still stand, but the structure was roofed in later in the century.

The Athenaeum, a stylistically exotic house designed for President Polk's nephew, Samuel Polk Walker, by Adolphus Heinman of Nashville, shows perhaps unconscious traces of the battle of styles. Heinman specialized in fanciful buildings. In the Athenaeum, basic Gothic forms are displayed in the crenelated

Washington Tomb, Mount Vernon, Virginia, 1831–39. A print published in 1841. (Virginia State Library)

The Athenaeum, Columbia, Tennessee, 1835–37

Marine hospital, Charleston, 1831–34

wings, the quatrefoil ornaments in the parapet of the central block, and the buttresses to either side of the first-floor arcade and at the corners of the wings; a Middle Eastern influence marks the arches and balustrades. In spite of its Saracenic–Gothic appearance, however, the house, in general form, follows the three-part Palladian scheme popularized in the South by Thomas Jefferson. It took its name from the school of which it became a part, and which it has outlasted, and now belongs to the Association for the Preservation of Tennessee Antiquities.

Even such skilled architects as Robert Mills (1781–1855) were not immune to the application of a little Gothic to add spice to their work. Trained under Jefferson and Latrobe, Mills expanded upon their flirtations with Gothic as a relief from the gravity of the Classical Revival. With a reputation for practical, solidly built public buildings, he was commissioned by the federal government to design two marine hospitals, one for New Orleans and one for Charleston. The Charleston hospital plans were similar to those for the slightly earlier New Orleans hospital. The brick building features a double-tier piazza between two projecting end pavilions, again recalling the Palladian idiom, but is given a relatively mild Gothic flavor by the large pointed arches of the end pavilions and the clustered columns of the piazza. The window and door transoms and iron railings are also highlighted with Gothic details. The building is now occupied by the Charleston Housing Authority.

CARPENTERS GOTHIC

New York Yacht Club, by A. J. Davis, 1845

EVOLVED DURING THE 1830s, Carpenters Gothic is a phenomenon unique to this country. The strong carpentry tradition in America, the demand for quickly constructed buildings, and the incredible abundance of fine timber combined to make wooden Gothic a natural development. Similar structures would have been unthinkable in nineteenth-century western Europe where wood was scarce and where such freedom with traditional architectural forms would not have been tolerated. Carpenters Gothic is distinguished chiefly by its profusion of sawn and carved details. The fact that most of these details were originally designed to be executed in stone did not deter American architects and carpenters from interpreting them in another material, an activity greatly facilitated by the introduction in the 1830s and '40s of more efficient sawing methods. Most notable of these was the steam-powered scroll saw which could quickly cut from thin boards the scrolled ornament so often associated with the style; most Carpenters Gothic is more or less based on designs from the many pattern-books published in mid-century, and was expressed in the exuberant application of wooden ornament to every sort of building.

One of the earliest important expressions of Carpenters Gothic is the Unitarian First Parish Church, facing the main entrance to the Harvard Yard. It is also, interestingly enough, an early example of a Gothic building essentially devoid of any Greek Revival or other Classical overtones. While most Carpenters Gothic structures were designed by the carpenters themselves with the help of pattern-books, this church was the work of the noted Massachusetts architect, Isaiah Rogers (1800–69), who built his reputation mainly as a designer of large

Greek Revival hotels. But Rogers was originally trained as a carpenter and worked at that trade for several years before becoming a professional architect. It is hardly surprising that one of his few churches should be a genuinely inspired work of wooden construction, if not of Gothic design. Unfortunately the building has lost most of its original rich ornamentation. Damaged in a storm in 1954, the tower's corner finials and crenelations were removed, and the sawn parapets lining the front gable, with the finials at the corners of the building, were stripped off during renovations, leaving the church with little of the fanciful character provided by its architect.

Beneath its Gothic embellishments, the famous Wedding Cake House in Kennebunk, Maine, is a brick structure built in 1826 in standard late Federal style. It received its "frosting" in 1855, shortly after the adjacent Gothic barn was erected. With its wooden spires, sawn spandrels, nailed crenelations, and boarded buttresses, the house has come to be regarded as the quintessence of Carpenters Gothic, even though it is not, technically, a pure example. The trim was designed and executed by the owner, George W. Bourne, whose descendants still own the house. Few American buildings have inspired more delight.

First Parish Church, Cambridge, 1833

Wedding Cake House, Kennebunk, Maine, as remodeled in 1855

AN EARNEST EFFORT

Plate VI from Essay on Gothic Architecture, *1836*

IF IT IS difficult to tell about many buildings of the 1830s whether they are more Gothic or more something else, the decade did see some sincere, if not always completely polished, attempts to give new buildings in the style a bit more purity. One contribution to this effort was the first book on Gothic architecture written and published in the United States. Its author, John Henry Hopkins, was not an architect but the first Protestant Episcopal bishop of Vermont. While serving as a priest in Pittsburgh, he had been frustrated by the dearth of suitable Gothic plans on which to model the church his parish was about to build. In the end he designed the building himself with the help of a volume of Britton's *Architectural Antiquities of Great Britain*, lent him by a friend. Hopkins later studied lithography and produced his own book on ecclesiastical Gothic architecture "designed chiefly for the use of the clergy." Among its lithographs Hopkins included not only his own designs but additional details taken from Augustus Charles Pugin (q.v.) and Britton. While the book is not the most sophisticated of architectural writings, it had considerable influence on church architecture of the period. In conformity with the attitude of the times, Hopkins showed more concern for the Romantic effect of the Gothic than with its structural logic. His comments on the plate shown here point out that the ceiling is perfectly flat, but "filled up with a representation in painting of Gothic tracery." Such fakery must have scandalized those later ecclesiastical architects who came under the far-reaching influence of that eccentric genius, Augustus Welby Northmore Pugin (1812–52).

A LOFTY STANDARD

Frontispiece, The True Principles of
Pointed or Christian Architecture, *1841*

THE FRONTISPIECE OF Pugin's *The True Principles of Pointed or Christian Architecture*, shown here, might well be a self-portrait of the author, who undertook his work as a holy endeavor, performed for the glory of God, and who not only awakened England to the beauties of Medieval design but played a significant role in educating American attitudes toward the Gothic style. In a room filled with religious objects, the architect, in monkish robes, piously produces his inspired designs.

Pugin's father, Augustus Charles Pugin, was a French émigré who in England became a draftsman and an expert on the Gothic style. He worked with John Nash, executing most of the firm's Gothic detailing, and beginning in 1821 published *Specimens of Gothic Architecture* with E. J. Willson; this work, widely read in England and America, contained measured drawings of many noted English buildings. From his father the younger Pugin received a thorough grounding in drawing and Medieval design. He developed a strong religious bent, and came to attach great symbolic and religious values to the Gothic style. He early grew impatient of what he felt was the apathy of the Church of England and its disregard of Medieval heritage, and in 1834 converted to Catholicism, declaring: "I feel perfectly convinced that the Roman Catholic Church is the only true one, and the only one in which the grand and sublime style of Church architecture can ever be restored."

To Pugin, his beloved Gothic was the product of Medieval Catholic society; only in the context of the "true faith" could an architect comprehend the essence of the style, and for him the principles governing Gothic design and the soul inherent in Gothic Medieval work could not be regained "but by a restoration of the ancient feelings and sentiments; 'tis they alone can restore Gothic architecture." He attributed the "decline of the arts" to the Reformation; because men were devout and good in the Middle Ages, they obviously built "good buildings."

Pugin fathered the idea, for long widely accepted, that architecture has morality, and that Gothic is the most moral of architectural styles. No matter what its aesthetic appeal, a building produced by a "bad" society must be a "bad" building. He also fostered an architectural ethic. He condemned the facadism of Renaissance buildings, ridiculing their false openings, imitation materials, and nonstructural ornamentation. This radical concept is summed up in *The True Principles*: "The two great rules for design are these. First, that there should be no features about a building which are not necessary for convenience, construction, or propriety; second, that all ornament should consist of enrichment of the essential construction of the building." Gothic took on an entirely new aspect in the light of Pugin's principles. He set a new and loftier standard, rendering all earlier Gothic Revival building old-fashioned. His theories are expressed in eight major books, and in the designs for over a hundred architectural works, all produced over an amazingly active seventeen years. (He did much of his drawing adrift in a little fishing boat.) But compressing the work of a century into less than twenty years took a sad toll: Pugin died mad at the age of forty.

His books, filled with extraordinarily beautiful drawings of buildings, carvings, metalwork, and furniture, swiftly found their way to America where they had an immediate impact on both architects and laymen. His theories on the moral and ethical nature of architecture appealed to the sophisticated, but his chief contribution to architectural development here lies in the lavishly illustrated descriptions which provided eager builders and designers with practical and inspiring guidance on Gothic modes and building methods. For a country without Medieval models, Pugin supplied directions on how to authentically construct, ornament, and furnish Gothic works. In such skilled hands as those of Richard Upjohn, James Renwick, and Minard Lafever (qq.v.), Pugin's books spurred the production of mature Gothic Revival buildings, devoid of the naivete which had characterized American Gothic since the eighteenth century.

MID-CENTURY CHURCHES

St. Peter's Church, Albany, by Upjohn, 1859–60

IN HIS LONG and productive career, Richard Upjohn (1802–78) gave this country some of its finest churches, and fully subscribed, insofar as he was able, to Pugin's demand for authenticity in Gothic church design. Born in England and trained as a cabinetmaker, Upjohn came to America in 1829, settling in New Bedford, Massachusetts, where he found employment as an architectural draftsman. He moved to Boston in 1833, and after working for a time in the office of the well-known architect Alexander Parris, set up his own practice. It was during the Boston years that he became seriously interested in the Gothic mode and started acquiring books on the subject. In one of his first important commissions (St. John's Church, Bangor, Maine, 1837–39) he strove for the archaeological accuracy of form and detail sought by his fellows in England.

He was catapulted into national fame when he fortuitously gained the commission to design a new church for what was probably the richest and best-known Episcopal parish in the country. In 1839 the second church of Trinity Parish, New York (q.v.), was seriously weakened by heavy snows, and the Corporation resolved to engage an architect to determine whether the building should be repaired or replaced. The selection committee first met in a room containing a lithograph of Upjohn's recently completed Bangor church, and a committeeman pointed out that whoever designed that church must know what he was doing. Happily, Dr. John Wainwright, Rector of Trinity, was able to identify the architect. Upjohn was thereupon called to New York, where inspection of the old building led him to conclude that it was beyond repair. The Corporation accordingly decided to have it pulled down and commissioned him to design a suitable replacement. By the time he started to work on the plans,

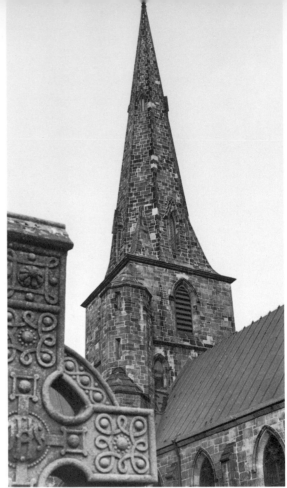

*Left, the third Trinity Church,
New York, 1841–46.
A bird's-eye view published in 1847.
(Museum of the City of New York)*

*Right, St. Mary's Church,
Burlington, New Jersey, 1846–48*

Upjohn had become acquainted with Pugin's publications on Gothic architecture. Thus armed with substantive knowledge of Medieval design, he was able to produce one of the purest and grandest specimens of the style yet seen in America, and the church provided an appropriate setting for the more ceremonial ritual then being reintroduced in the Anglican Communion. Pugin's influence is shown in Trinity's exterior scheme which bears a striking resemblance to "An Ideal Church," a design in the Perpendicular style from *The True Principles.*

Completed in 1846, Trinity was considered a marvel. Although purists criticized its plaster vaulting, no Gothic edifice so splendid in concept, authentic in design, and rich in crafted details had yet been seen here. It secured Upjohn's reputation, but was not much imitated, as it was too large and expensive for any but the richest parishes to copy. Furthermore, the Early English and Decorated styles soon came to be advanced as more appropriate for Episcopal churches than the Perpendicular.

This reversion to earlier Gothic forms, followed by Upjohn in subsequent works, was largely initiated by the Cambridge Camden Society, founded in England for the advancement of Medieval art and architecture. It was deeply concerned with the quality of modern church architecture and one of its chief activities was the promotion of the simple Early English parish church as the model for new houses of worship. The Society's reverence for Gothic buildings was summed up by the Rev. George Ayliffe Poole: "A Gothic Church, in its perfection, is an exposition of the distinctive doctrines of Christianity, clothed upon with a material form; and is, as Coleridge has more forcibly expressed it, 'the petrification of our religion.'" The Cambridge Camden Society held that a

60

revival of the building arts of the Middle Ages would serve not only to improve standards of architectural quality and taste, but to remind the beholder of the verities of Christian religion. It remained, however, firmly Anglican, with no thought that a reversion to Catholicism was necessary to achieve its aims.

The members of the Society identified themselves as "Ecclesiologists," and beginning in 1841 they published *The Ecclesiologist*, a periodical devoted to church building, restoration, ritual, and symbolism. A primary purpose was to propagate the aims of the Society throughout the English-speaking world. The Society received its biggest boost in this country when the Rt. Rev. George Washington Doane, Bishop of New Jersey, was elected a patron member. Bishop Doane's profound interest in architecture led him to promote the first church buildings in America in which an attempt was made to conform to Ecclesiological standards. The first of these was the Chapel of the Holy Innocents (1845–46), a simple stone building designed by John Notman (q.v.) for a girls' school in Burlington, New Jersey. This was followed by St. Mary's Church, a handsome brown sandstone edifice in the Early English style, commissioned of Upjohn by the bishop. St. Mary's was the first American church convincingly patterned after a specific English model; it is based on St. John Baptist, Shottesbrook, a Medieval church in Berkshire. Upjohn's skillful handling of its materials and architectural elements brought the religious side of the Gothic Revival in America to maturity. The stone steeple became a hallmark of sophisticated church design.

The renown accruing from Trinity and St. Mary's brought Upjohn commissions for Gothic churches all over the country. Nearly all of these were executed in the Early English or Decorated style and were characterized by the accurate historicism advocated by the Ecclesiologists. Among his more notable achievements are Christ Church, Raleigh (1848–54), St. Paul's Church, Buffalo (1850–51), St. Peter's Church, Albany (1859–60), Central Congregational Church, Boston (1865–67), and the now-destroyed St. Thomas' Church, New York (1868–70). Upjohn did not limit his practice to impressive masonry urban churches; indeed, he felt strongly that good design should be available for simple churches, chapels, and missions. He therefore accepted commissions without fee for rural wooden meetinghouses, and in 1852 published *Upjohn's Rural Architecture*, which contains designs for board-and-batten churches, parsonages, and schoolhouses to be built at minimum expense. A characteristic expression of Upjohn's work in this mode is the chapel of St. Mary's Junior College in Raleigh, which moved the local bishop to declare: "I was gratified by its beauty, its appropriate arrangements, and its adaptation to its purpose."

Gothic churches do not comprise the whole of Upjohn's oeuvre; he produced some uncommonly fine residences and public buildings, mostly in the Tuscan mode. Yet beyond these creditable ventures in other forms, Upjohn's authorship of Trinity Church, his role in the Ecclesiological movement, and the consistently high quality of his religious buildings indisputably rank him as the leading Gothic Revival church architect of nineteenth-century America.

Left, St. Mary's Junior College, Raleigh, 1855, the chapel

Right, Chapel of the Cross, Madison County, Mississippi, 1850–52

The English Ecclesiologist influence and the growth of the Episcopal denomination in the 1840s led to the founding in 1847 of the New York Ecclesiological Society, American counterpart of the Cambridge Camden Society. This organization immediately started the *New York Ecclesiologist*, a journal intended to disseminate Ecclesiological precepts and educate the Episcopal clergy in church architecture, history, and liturgical tradition. The lack of architectural purity in many new churches outside eastern metropolitan areas prompted the American Society to try to control quality in Gothic design by recommending the Early English parish church as the most suitable model for religious edifices. One of the Medieval churches most admired by the English Ecclesiologists which appeared to have a design particularly adaptable to American needs was St. Michael's Long Staunton (ca. 1230), a quaint Early English church near Cambridge. Drawings of this building provided the basis for the design of the highly significant St. James the Less, a modest but exquisitely crafted Philadelphia church completed in 1849, and the first American structure to have both its design and execution directly supervised by the English Ecclesiologists. It set a precedent and a standard for Gothic parish churches of the mid-nineteenth century.

As soon as it came into existence, the New York Ecclesiological Society began to receive multitudinous requests for church designs from all parts of the country. Many were answered by the Society's first official architect, Frank Wills (d. 1856), and by virtue of this position Wills became an extremely influential church designer. Only recently, however, has he received the credit he deserves for improving the quality of mid-nineteenth-century ecclesiastical design. English by birth, he acquired a specialized knowledge of church architecture through his association with the Exeter [England] Diocesan Architectural Society and its founder, the Rev. John Medley, whose notions of Gothic Revival conformed to those of the Cambridge Camden Society. In 1845, when Medley became the first Bishop of New Brunswick, Canada, Wills followed him and supervised the construction of the new cathedral. He left New Brunswick in 1848 and moved to New York, where his reputation as an architect of ecclesiologically correct churches gained him his position with the New York Ecclesiological Society.

62

Church of the Holy Trinity, Brooklyn, 1844–47. (Museum of the City of New York)

Wills supplied parish church designs through both the Society and his own New York architectural office. The circumstances by which he obtained the commission for the Chapel of the Cross in Mississippi are not perfectly clear, although his identification as the architect is supported by local tradition and by a reference in the *New York Ecclesiologist*. The building is not ranked among Wills's major works, but its simplicity and refinement make it a cogent example of what the Ecclesiologists were trying to accomplish. Save that it is built of brick rather than stone, the Chapel of the Cross is closely patterned after St. Michael's Long Staunton and includes the characteristic bell cote, buttressed end, side-porch entrance, and simple lancet openings. Although it lacks the refined masonry detailing of St. James the Less, it does illustrate that good design based on sound Ecclesiological principles may be found even in so remote a spot as central Mississippi. Erected by Mrs. Margaret L. Johnstone as a memorial to her husband, the church was visited in 1851 by the Rt. Rev. William Mercer Green, first Bishop of Mississippi, who called it "one of the most beautiful structures of the Church kind to be found in any of our Southern or Western dioceses."

The Church of the Holy Trinity in Brooklyn, like Upjohn's New York Trinity, is an expression of deepened religious fervor in the Episcopal Church and

63

its revived consciousness of the Medieval heritage. It also is a conspicuous symbol of one man's pride in his neighborhood. The ambitious structure, designed by Minard Lafever (1798–1854), was the dream of Edgar John Bartow, a prosperous paper manufacturer who wanted to crown the highest point in Brooklyn Heights with the largest and finest church in the city. It was not exactly an offering to the Church, for Bartow leased it to the vestry, who were not able to purchase it until 1856. Bartow exercised a strong influence on the design and kept prodding Lafever to make it more elaborate. As the view of the interior shows, it is a sumptuous example of the English Decorated style, the nave dominated by a handsome vaulted ceiling enriched by short lierne ribs. The foliated capitals, Flamboyant tracery, and intricately detailed organ loft and case add to the effect.

Lafever's Gothic was more freely interpreted than that of most of his contemporaries; his were original compositions which did not follow the specific Medieval examples advocated by the Ecclesiologists. Large Gothic buildings compose the most significant part of his output, but his renown is rather based on the authorship of five pattern-books that deal primarily with the Grecian style.

Not all Gothic Revival church architects were touched by the Ecclesiologists; there were those who continued to work in their favorite Perpendicular and Tudor styles. But in spite of the popularity of the Tudor style, few were ambitious enough to attempt its most characteristic feature, fan vaulting. The Charleston architect Francis D. Lee (1826–85), created an exception: a magnificent fan-vaulted ceiling which is part of the scheme that gothicized the Unitarian Church in Charleston. His efforts are the more praiseworthy in that he was constrained to work within existing walls. The form of the fan vaulting and pendants closely follows Henry VII's Chapel in Westminster Abbey (1503–19), although the span is much narrower, and the vaulting is not perfectly genuine inasmuch as it is lath and plaster rather than stone. Originally the organ was free standing, allowing light from the west window to enter the nave. Like many

St. John's Church, Buffalo,
1846–48. (Frank Leslie's Illustrated
Newspaper, *March 29, 1856*)

architects of his era, Lee was sufficiently versatile to design in a variety of historic
styles. He is perhaps best known for his Farmers and Exchange Bank (1853–59),
an exercise in the Moorish style on Charleston's East Bay.

When St. John's Church, Buffalo, was burned as the result of a rocket alighting
on the bell tower during the course of the Glorious Fourth celebrations of 1868, a
Gothic and city landmark was lost. The *Buffalo Courier* mourned: "The tower
. . . was the first object visible in approaching Buffalo by the lake, so that instead
of the shapely pile which once served him as a beacon on the shore, the sailor will
now descry but an unshapely ruin." The *Morning Express*, castigating the fire
department for its dilatory arrival and inability to mount enough water pressure
(without bursting the hoses) to reach the site of the blaze, described the building
as "one of the most chaste and stately specimens of church architecture. . . ."
Designed by Calvin N. Otis, St. John's boasted the first open timber roof in
America "supported wholly upon hammer beams and spandrels." The awesome
structure was composed of six independent trusses and two half-trusses and had a
61½-foot span. The overall height of the interior space was 61 feet. The quantities
of virgin timber still available in America made such a roof perfectly practicable,
but that a properly constructed hammer-beam ceiling should have been put up at

65

this relatively early date demonstrates the increasing attention paid by American architects to Gothic structural systems as opposed to superimposed ornamentation.

James Renwick, Jr. (1818–95), earned his reputation for competence in the Gothic style with his design for New York's Grace Church (1843–46), a scheme he produced when only twenty-five years old. With youthful spontaneity he achieved a lively masterpiece in the English taste that would have excited the admiration of Pugin. The fame of this work led to commissions from other prosperous congregations and ultimately landed him the one that climaxed his career, St. Patrick's Cathedral. That the most influential Roman Catholic archdiocese in the country should select a Protestant architect to execute its seat and symbol is illustrative of Renwick's skill and renown. The commission for the biggest church building erected in the United States up to that time was somewhat overwhelming, but Renwick deftly produced a suitably majestic scheme.

His plans, begun in 1853, called for a building combining French, German, and English elements; the diverse nationalities represented in the diocese dictated that he divagate from the strictly English format to which he had adhered in previous designs. Although a direct connection has not been established, Renwick may have derived inspiration from the markedly similar Sainte-Clotilde, a large church in Paris begun in 1846 under the aegis of architect F. C. Gau, a German trained under a French master. A landmark of continental Gothic Revival, Sainte-Clotilde was a popular model for large Catholic churches, well known in Catholic circles, and Renwick may have been steering a safe course by generally acknowledging a design that had already met the approval of the hierarchy.

The continental aspect of St. Patrick's is evident mainly in its exterior and plan. The three-portal facade with its great rose window is distinctly French, while the "stone lace" ornamentation of the tapered twin spires combines French and German elements. The plan, with shallow transepts and ambulatory, follows the classic French pattern. The interior, however, is generally English Decorated in its detailing and is dominated by magnificent English stellar vaulting rising 112 feet to the ridge rib.

The Cathedral was formally opened in 1879 and the spires, completed in 1888, dominated mid-town Manhattan's skyline for some fifty years until dwarfed by Rockefeller Center just across Fifth Avenue. Since its opening St. Patrick's has served in the fullest sense as a great urban cathedral. A cool haven from the aggressive commercialism without, the cavernous interior is always gently astir with the flickering of banks of candles, the murmur of masses, and the coming and going of tourists and the devout. In addition to its day-to-day service it provides a matchless setting for great religious ceremonies, from the funerals of national figures to the visit of a reigning Pope. The late Cardinal Francis J. Spellman expressed its essence: "The grandeur of this holy place has lifted up the lowly and taught humility to the mighty. At its portals, the world seems left behind."

66

St. Patrick's Cathedral, New York, 1858–78, 1888. (Art Journal, *1876*)

St. Patrick's occupies a special place in American Gothic Revival, for it marks the first project in this country of a magnitude comparable to anything being done in Europe. With it the United States emerged from its provincial status in the Revival and took its place in the front rank. Although sometimes accused of a certain stiffness, Renwick's masterpiece demonstrates that Americans were capable of accomplishing work of a high order and on the grandest scale, opening the way for such awesome projects as the Cathedral Church of St. John the Divine and the Washington Cathedral.

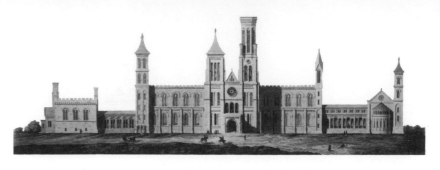

Smithsonian Institution, Norman scheme as built, by Renwick, 1846. (Smithsonian Institution)

THE SMITHSONIAN COMPETITION

IN 1846 A notice appeared in the Washington papers inviting interested architects to submit designs for a "suitable building" for the newly established Smithsonian Institution. A dozen architects did so, offering schemes in either the fashionable Gothic Revival or the less popular Romanesque. Among them were John Notman, John Haviland, Wells and Arnot, Isaiah Rogers, Owen G. Warren, and James Renwick, Jr. Renwick submitted designs in both styles, and his Norman scheme was declared the winner. It was amid a storm of protest, however, that the choice was announced, as his design had apparently been selected not only before the stated closing date but even before all the other entries had been received. In spite of accusations of favoritism and illegality, and demands for a fresh competition, the election stood, and construction on the building started in 1847.

It appears that Renwick's champion on the executive committee of the Smithsonian was Robert Dale Owen of Indiana, eldest son of that Robert Owen who founded the utopian New Harmony colony. Representative Owen had forwarded to his brother, the geologist Dr. David Dale Owen, a proposed plan for a similar institution, drawn by Robert Mills in 1841, requesting suggestions and guidelines for the officers and regents who were to judge the competition. He declared a preference for the "simple forms" of the "Pure Norman," and wrote: "My chief inducement to apply to you in preference to a regularly bred architect is that I know you will consult utility first, in the various internal arrangements, and let architectural elegance follow, as a secondary, though not unimportant consideration." Dr. Owen recommended a late twelfth-century mode, Norman, which employed occasional pointed arches, as being economical, allowing of the introduction of all sorts of modern conveniences and having a simplicity and massiveness appropriate to a public building. He also pointed out the advantages of skylights for both exhibition and lecture rooms.

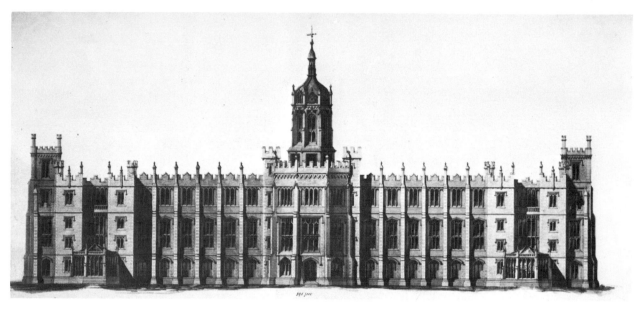

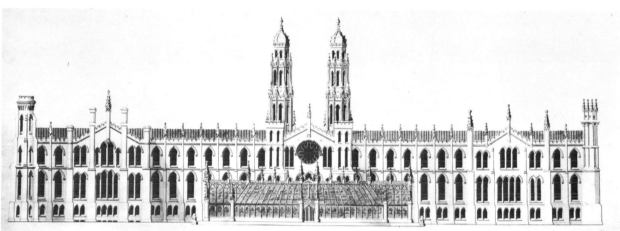

Smithsonian competition. Top to bottom.
John Notman's entry; Owen G. Warren's entry;
Warren's entry, east end. (Smithsonian Institution)

The competing architects all had the benefit of Dr. Owen's reflections on civic architecture, and in addition were directed to design the whole building "reasonably" fireproof. Oddly enough, Renwick's winning design ignored the recommendations for overhead lighting, was so far from fireproof as to have both wooden floors and timber roofs, and required alterations in plan to secure the specified spaces. The design, however, was unquestionably Norman.

Preserved in the Smithsonian archives are Renwick's original Norman design and a number of the rejected Gothic entries, including Renwick's. The central portion at least of his unused scheme apparently was not wholly wasted effort, as

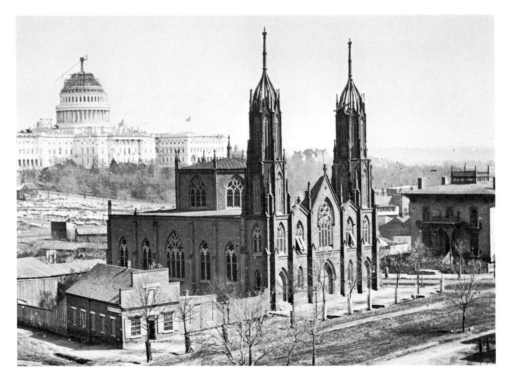

*Smithsonian competition,
Renwick's Gothic entry.
(Smithsonian Institution)*

*Trinity Church,
Washington, D.C., 1849–51*

he appears to have used it without charge, for the facade of Trinity Church, Washington. This impressive structure was built on land near the Capitol donated by William Wilson Corcoran, for whom Renwick later designed the chapel of Oak Hill Cemetery (1850), Georgetown, and what is now the Renwick Gallery (1859–60). With the deterioration of the neighborhood at the time of the First World War Trinity began to go rapidly downhill and was ultimately abandoned by the congregation. It was last used as a social service center for what had become a slum neighborhood, and was demolished about 1930.

70

A FAMILY'S FANCIES

Bremo slave chapel,
Fluvanna County, Virginia, 1835

THE COCKE FAMILY of Virginia produced at least two generations of patrons and amateur architects, and both John Hartwell Cocke (1780–1866) and his son Philip St. George Cocke (1809–61) were sufficiently taken with the Gothic mood and flavor to erect a variety of buildings in that style. From the tidewater, where the family had settled in the seventeenth century, John Cocke moved to Bremo, the family land grant in Fluvanna County, in 1809. He first built a simple frame cottage, later known as Bremo Recess, and from then on the plantation was the stage for his seemingly endless architectural activities, including the Palladian barn and the great Roman Revival mansion, completed in 1820 (see Desmond Guinness and Julius Trousdale Sadler, Jr., *Mr. Jefferson, Architect*). As the spirit of the Gothic Revival rose, General Cocke built in that mode a chapel for his slaves, enlarged and embellished Lower Bremo in Gothic style for his son Cary, and, in 1844, remodeled Bremo Recess. He encased the house in a Jacobean shell into which he introduced a Gothic arcaded porch and gothicized "Palladian" windows. It is said that the Jacobean theme was to commemorate the reign in which the original Bremo land grant was given, and the Palladian motif was Cocke's architectural signature. In 1844 he described the remodeled house in the *Richmond Enquirer*: "The style is copied from . . . the well-remembered old six-chimney house in Williamsburg, once the property of the Custis family, and 'Bacon's Castle' in Surry." There are certainly no pointed arches at Bacon's Castle, but Cocke may have felt that an emphatic historical note would enhance the antique or romantic mood at Bremo Recess.

In the year after Bremo Recess received its new aspect, General Cocke's son, Philip St. George Cocke, began the construction of Belmead, on the heights above the James midway between Bremo and Richmond. Philip had married a considerable heiress, and was one of the richest men in the South, with extensive Virginia properties, but lacked a suitable manorial residence. Upon retiring from

Bremo Recess,
as remodeled in 1844.
Right, east gable.

the army in 1834, he left his last post of Charleston, and having lived for a short space in Surry County, settled in Powhatan County. The design for Belmead was provided by A. J. Davis, who for the first time in his practice included printed specifications with his drawings, in order to give himself firmer control of a project so far from his office.

Cocke's strong predilection for the Gothic style must have been fostered by his father, and he may have been familiar with such publications as *Mansions of England in the Olden Time* (1839–49) by Joseph Nash, or perhaps with Davis's own *Rural Residences, Etc.*, of 1837, which was "To be had of the architect and of Booksellers generally throughout the United States." *Rural Residences* contains an illustration of Blithewood, a villa overlooking the Hudson in Dutchess County, New York, of which Davis writes: "The design is irregular and suited to scenery of a picturesque character and to an eminence commanding an extensive prospect. . . . This house should be built of stone or brick, stuccoed in imitation of stone, having marble or light colored free-stone trimmings. The bay windows and oriel of wood, painted and dusted with pulverized marble or grained in imitation of oak. The entrance porch might be either of stone or wood. The battlements and gable with its crockets might be of wood, painted to match the stone, as well as all tracery in window frames, bays, and oriels." The description might be of Belmead. Within Belmead there are marble mantels of Gothic design, and in the windows of the major rooms appear occasional panes of colored glass, bearing painted likenesses of the crops grown on the plantation.

Belmead was the first James River plantation house to be built in the Gothic taste. It was not universally popular; a relative described it as "a huge costly affair—an ugly barn of a place," but its beauty in the eye of the beholder has appreciated over the years. In the lean period after the Civil War the house passed out of the family, and in 1897 it was turned into a Catholic training school, St. Emma's Industrial and Agricultural Institute. The Institute has closed, and most of the school buildings have been razed, but the house is still owned and occupied by the Sisters of the Blessed Sacrament.

Founded in 1839, the Virginia Military Institute was originally housed in a somewhat dilapidated building north of Lexington, and within a few years it became apparent to the Board of Visitors, of which Philip Cocke was a member, that a long-range building program was a necessity. Belmead was going up at that time, and it was undoubtedly Cocke who suggested that A. J. Davis be employed on the undertaking; indeed, Cocke was very likely largely responsible for the character of the "adequate and tasteful design" which Davis subsequently submitted, for the suggestions sent to Davis by Supt. Francis Smith in the summer of 1848 are strongly reminiscent of the Citadel (1829–32) in Charleston, Cocke's last army post. Davis's original studies for a Gothic campus were well received. In response to his request for further guidance, Smith proposed that the barracks stand four stories high around a quadrangle, and house lecture rooms, debating rooms, a chemical laboratory, and a library; the cadets' rooms were to provide living space for two or three students apiece, and to open "upon piazzas in the inside." Davis planned for "piazzas" on three sides of the court, echoing the arcades of the Citadel, and the typical Town and Davis grouped windows deemphasize the height of the building, so that its four stories resemble the Citadel's two, but the central gateway with its twin towers is far more elaborate than the entrance to the Citadel.

In 1850 Davis traveled to Virginia, visiting the nearly completed Belmead, and going to Lexington to settle on the location of various buildings at the Institute. Cocke reported to Superintendent Smith that he was "quite pleased with Davis' plan. The castellated and battlemented Gothic style which he adopted is most suitable for military buildings and is the plainest and cheapest style we could have selected." With this design Davis established a model much imitated in military school architecture, as at Fishburne Military School in Waynesboro, Virginia, and Culver Military Academy, Culver, Indiana.

Funds for the purpose were at last allocated, and in 1851 the south front was completed. In the following nine years other building were put up as monies became available, and a start was made on the two Barracks wings to the north. The Civil War halted this construction, which would have completed the quadrangle, and in 1864 a fire set by Union troops left most of the Institute in

Left, Belmead, Powhatan County, Virginia, 1845–52.
An early photograph.
(John Page Elliott Collection)

Right, plan by Davis for "Mansion of 'Belmead', James River, Va. Erected for P. St. G. Cocke, 1845."
(Metropolitan Museum of Art, Harris Brisbane Dick Fund, 1924)

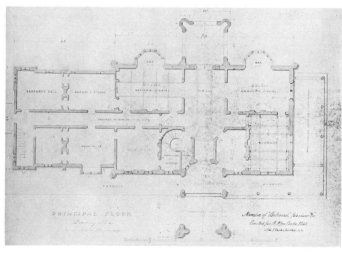

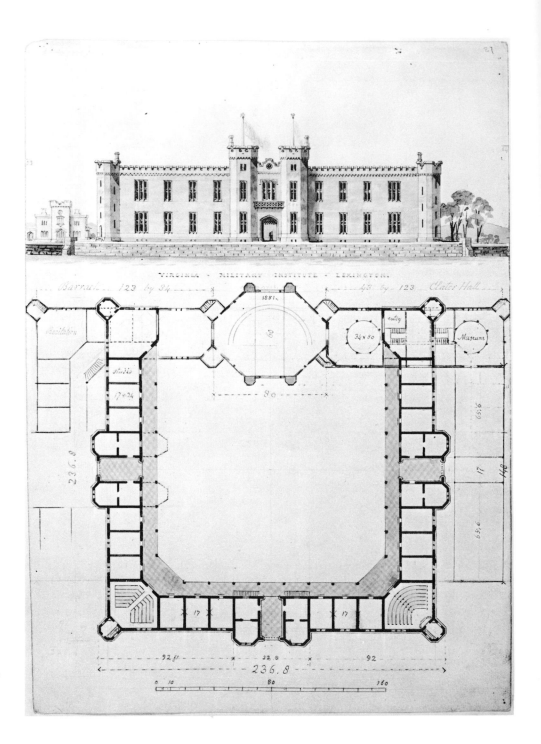

Virginia Military Institute, Lexington, elevation and plan by Davis, 1850. (Metropolitan Museum of Art, Harris Brisbane Dick Fund, 1924)

ruins. In the late '60s the original buildings were reconstructed, but there were no funds in battle-drained Virginia to complete the north Barracks or to carry out the rest of Davis's designs. It was not until 1914, when Bertram Grosvenor Goodhue (q.v.) was commissioned to unify the structures at the Institute, that further work was put in train, and by 1923 the Barracks had at last become the enclosed quadrangle it was intended to be. In the late 1940s the New Barracks was added; the elevation adheres closely to Davis's original design for the south front.

74

MID-CENTURY HOUSES

Oatlands, Queens, New York, as remodeled in 1838.
(The Spur, April 1935)

IN THE 1830s historical eclecticism established its position in American architectural development. The Greek Revival continued dominant, but the spate of geographical, historical, and architectural publications from abroad whetted public appetite for visual variety and romantic associations in their buildings. Architects and builders began to experiment with a myriad of styles. The next twenty years saw the production of public, residential, ecclesiastical, and commercial buildings clothed in historical and regional guises ranging from Roman to Persian, from Renaissance to Swiss. One critic observed that there appeared to be nothing that people would not try; A. J. Davis averred that he had planned buildings in fourteen different styles.

Throughout, the Gothic steadily increased in popularity. Andrew Jackson Downing's strictures on the obsession for squeezing everything into a Greek temple, Scott's glorification of the Middle Ages, and critical ridicule of the more bizarre modes, all contributed to its success. The style had qualities that fulfilled the aspirations of the era: never monotonous, it was hailed as bold, candid, and lofty. Unlike the Classical modes, with their rigid rules of orders and proportions, the Gothic encouraged inventiveness, and adventurous creativity was an important by-product of the Romantic spirit.

Although Gothic Revival churches in varying degrees of authenticity had been built on and off in this country since the eighteenth century, until the 1830s the style was very rarely used for residences. Then came the flood, and Camelot was a rage. Castles described by one foreign visitor as "very young" began to dot the landscape. In 1836 a traveler on the new Camden and Amboy Railroad said of his

75

journey along the Delaware: "New and beautiful scenes continually opened to view—with fine country seats, built in imitation Gothic castles, with towers and battlements standing amid a fine growth of trees of every kind."

This tide of Gothic housing was mostly of wood, put up without much regard to the accurate use of appropriate motifs. Ecclesiastical, military, and domestic forms, executed with only a hazy resemblance to their models, were indiscriminately mixed in residential work. Delightful as these New World Strawberry Hills may have been, stricter Gothicists criticized them severely. This ultimately led to public contempt, and finally indifference, so that few of these naive and exuberant first attempts survive. Oatlands (formerly the Turf and Field Club at Belmont Park), a gingerbread castle torn down by the New York Racing Association, is a case in point. Those that do remain are largely substantial and restrained examples, most notably Oaklands, the stone-built, towered, and battlemented seat of the Gardiner family, in Gardiner, Maine, built in 1835–36 from Upjohn's designs.

Roseland, Woodstock,
Connecticut, 1846,
east elevation

These houses avoided the set formulas followed in many contemporary churches. Davis's designs and Downing's writings markedly raised the level of scholarship and consistency in Gothic house design, but their influence did not become nationwide until the mid-1850s; houses built outside their sphere remained subject to considerable caprice. Much of this inconsistency may be attributed to the lack of authentic models. The Middle Ages produced either large castles or humble vernacular cottages. There is no Medieval example of a middle-class suburban villa, and the mansions of the Tudor period are vast, rambling affairs, far too big to be copied. Imagination, as much as taste or scholarship, was required to tailor Medieval forms to Victorian living standards, and the results show a bewildering variety of interpretations of the Gothic home.

Roseland, so called for the rose gardens that once surrounded the house, is affectionately known as the Pink House from the insouciant color of its walls and molded Gothic chimney stacks of glazed stoneware. The oriel window, trellised porches, bargeboards, pinnacles, and crockets are accents of dark red, and the fence across the front of the lot, the pickets of which are carved to match the woodwork of the porches, is painted white. Roseland was built in 1846 as a summer residence for Henry Chandler Bowen, co-founder and later owner of *The Independent*, by Joseph C. Wells, the New York architect who designed the First Presbyterian Church (1846) standing on Fifth Avenue between Eleventh and Twelfth Streets in Manhattan. Wells was also responsible for the window seats in the deep bay windows of the twin parlors and the matching chairs and settee, which echo the motifs of the exterior trim. A ledger, still in the house, shows that this furniture was executed by Thomas Brooks of Brooklyn, who had also crafted pieces for the Bowens' Brooklyn Heights home. The main entrance of Roseland is under the south porte cochere; on the east the conservatory faces the street between the porches behind which lie the parlors. This enchanting example of Carpenters Gothic, maintained for generations by the Bowen family, is now under the care of the Society for the Preservation of New England Antiquities.

Roseland, the front parlor and the bowling alley in the barn

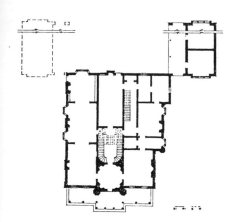

Staunton Hill, Charlotte County, Virginia, 1848. River front, detail of library bookcase, and plan.

When Charles Bruce built Staunton Hill in 1848, the "superior" Greek had been supplanted by the Gothic as fashion's darling, although just ten years before, his brother James had built Berry Hill, Halifax County, in the purest of Greek Revival. The disparate styles of these two family mansions exemplify the abrupt change in American taste. Bruce commissioned John E. Johnson to design his house, and departed on a Grand Tour. Eighteen months later, with a new bride, he moved into his mansion. Staunton Hill, with its accented entrance and center hall, and a range of rooms to either side, avoids the asymmetrical massing that characterized many of the later Gothic houses. The exterior is much in the castellated style, but a domestic touch is introduced in the elegant piazza of gray Italian marble which contrasts with the somewhat severe stuccoed walls. The piazza's marble floor continues into an octagonal entrance hall where Gothic ribs form a tent ceiling beneath which four niches house classical sculptures. The Gothic detailing in the marble mantels of the drawing rooms and library is complemented by Gothic motifs in the doors and plaster cornices; on the drawing room walls hang four identical Gothic mirrors, made in Venice, reflecting one another into infinity. The focal point of the library is the oriel window overlooking the rear court; its casements are separated by clustered collonettes similar to those marking the divisions of the room's crenelated bookcases. The upper floors are reached by a divided stair, the balustrade of which is formed by small Gothic arches, and on the third story is a great traceried window facing the Staunton River.

Staunton Hill was once a three-day's carriage drive from Richmond. The skilled workmen employed on the house, and much of the materials used in its construction, were brought from Philadelphia by water, from Albemarle Sound up the Roanoke and Staunton Rivers. The river was likewise the preferred highway for visitors. Today, when one approaches Staunton Hill by motor, the entrance is through the rear court formed by a long service wing and a balancing modern guest wing; the age of the automobile has, in effect, turned the house around. Only when approaching the house from the river does one see the little Gothic cottage to the left which was built to house the plantation office, the billiard room, and occasional strangers. Staunton Hill is still a Bruce family home.

In the Deep South, elaborate Gothic plantation houses were a rarity; up until the Civil War, planters much preferred the porticoes of the stately Greek Revival style, which was better suited to hot climates. Afton Villa not only was exceptional in the South, it was one of the most ornate of all mid-nineteenth-century American houses. In deference to its locale, the facade was shaded by a two-story portico, but one composed of clustered columns, pointed arches, openwork spandrels, and large pendants, all of wood. The house actually incorporated an earlier dwelling, and received its Gothic elaboration in the course

Afton Villa, West Feliciana Parish, Louisiana, 1849

Errolton, Columbus, Mississippi, ca. 1850

of an enlargement and remodeling carried out in 1849 by its owner, David Barrow, to please his Kentucky bride, Susan Woolfolk. Barrow family tradition has it that she had acquired an appreciation for Gothic architecture from the Waverley novels. The house was completely destroyed by fire in 1963.

In another atypical case, the citizens of Columbus, Mississippi, found that they could have the best of both stylistic worlds simply by substituting Gothic columns for Greek ones, and by adding some Gothic arches and scroll-sawn spandrels. These curious "Gothic" porticoes, each with slight variations, shade the facades of several otherwise ordinary antebellum houses in this southern town, such as Errolton, shown on the preceding page.

North or South, Gothic residences of the 1850s mostly took the form of rural villas or cottages. The Green–Meldrim House in Savannah is one of the rare free-standing urban mansions. Designed by John S. Norris of New York, the house was built for Charles Green, grandfather of Julien Green, the French–American author. The house lacks the characteristic steep gables of the villas and cottages; rather, its crenelated parapet lends it a castellated appearance. The fortified aspect is counterbalanced by the domestic iron veranda skirting the first floor. During the Civil War Gen. William T. Sherman destroyed almost everything in his path between Atlanta and the sea, but he spared the Green–Meldrim house, which he used as his headquarters. Perhaps he felt an affinity for its slightly martial character.

80

By adding units and increasing scale, an owner or builder could easily expand a Gothic cottage into a mansion; the Moses Fowler House, home of a successful Indiana businessman, is an example. More architecturally aware than most laymen, Fowler designed the house himself. The richly detailed dwelling is now owned by the Tippecanoe County Historical Association and is a museum.

Even a cattleman's homestead, in the days when a ranch house was a home on the range, could perfectly well take the form of a Gothic villa. The galleried and gabled mixture of Gothic and Italianate forms known as the John Marsh House was built for a native of Danvers, Massachusetts, who came to California to practice medicine. A true frontier "operator," Marsh charged a steer a mile for house calls, and amassed a sizable herd in a very short time. His new rank of cattle baron persuaded him to build a house worthy of his station, and he commissioned Thomas Boyd of San Francisco to design a suitably baronial seat. Although not on a par architecturally with eastern villas, Boyd's asymmetrical facade, crenelated tower, and Gothic verandas give the house an appealing individuality. An article in the *San Francisco Evening Bulletin* in 1856 describes its quality: "The architect . . . with true artistic perception of the beauty of the site, and of what was wanted in the building to make it harmonize with the surrounding scenery, has departed from the stereotyped square box . . . and has adopted the old English domestic style of architecture—a pleasing and appropriate union of Manor House and Castle." Dr. Marsh was murdered in a robbery shortly after the house was completed, and the estate soon went downhill. Owned today by the county, the boarded-up house is abandoned and deteriorating.

Left, Moses Fowler House, Lafayette, Indiana, 1851–52

Right, John Marsh House, Brentwood, California, 1853–56

Doghouse, Bangor, Maine, 1847

MID-CENTURY ARCHITECTS, designers, and builders were not content to gothicize only obvious structures such as houses and churches. To their way of thinking, the style was as appropriate for a locomotive or a kennel as for a state capitol, and anything that could be made Gothic was made Gothic. Just as we have our Colonial gas stations and pedimented shopping centers, the Victorians attached their Gothic to the most incongruous objects; the reduction of fashion to absurdity is a recurrent phenomenon. The mania for Gothic lasted until after the Civil War. The urban and rural landscapes sprouted Gothic barns, bridges, depots, factories, fences, jails, shelters, and shops, expressed in traditional brick, stone, or wood as well as in the more modern cast iron and concrete. A man could be born in a Gothic bed, receive baptism in a Gothic church, attend a Gothic school, live in a Gothic house, and at last be buried in a Gothic cemetery from a Gothic mortuary chapel.

Sophisticated opinion at last rebelled against this overweening Gothicism; architectural and social critics combined to ridicule its blithe lack of discrimination, and although their strictures did not cause the style to be abandoned, they did inhibit its use. As the Gothic tide ebbed, architects and designers tended to confine it to more conservative purposes and to give it a graver and more scholarly aspect. But by this time the country had been endowed with a plethora of delightful caprices, all serving to illustrate our ability to overdo a good thing.

The lengths to which Americans of the 1850s were prepared to go in medievalizing their surroundings were fully apparent in the Church Street Station in Nashville. Trains entered the passenger shed through two Saracenic arches, and all the corners of the building were guarded by octagonal turrets. Fit more for the Crusades than for modern warfare, the station had been damaged by shellfire when this photograph was taken during the Civil War. Later enlarged, it was eventually razed to make way for the present station, which opened in 1900.

82

Church Street Station,
Nashville, ca. 1854

The Auburn,
an 1854 express locomotive.
(Smithsonian Institution)

Floating Church of Our Saviour for Seamen, New York, 1844. (University of Virginia)

Gothic architecture was not confined to solid ground, as demonstrated by the floating seaport churches. These consecrated craft were launched with the idea of making religion more accessible to sailors, and there was no mistaking the function such gospel ships were intended to perform. The Floating Church of our Saviour for Seamen, New York, was supported on twin hulls and moored in the East River. A similar vessel, the Floating Church of the Redeemer (1849), was a familiar landmark in the Philadelphia harbor.

The prodigious Scott Memorial in Edinburgh was only the first of the towering Gothic pinnacles erected in honor of national heroes, but Calvin Pollard's projected Washington Monument for New York would have dwarfed them all. Like many another conception of such overwhelming scale, it was never realized. Presaging the skyscraper, the plans called for a gargantuan pentagonal tower, encrusted with ornament, to rise 425 feet above Union Square. Though undeniably bizarre, the scheme shows that, at least to some, the Gothic was acceptable for probably the most ambitious memorial yet planned in the United States. "The noblest monument in the known world," the *New York Herald Tribune* called it. It was not, however, acceptable to all. When the Washington

84

Monument Association announced the selection of Pollard's proposal, there was a storm of protest: "preposterous," "wretched stuff," and "the very sublime of nonsense" were some of the milder epithets. Unsolicited designs, mostly in a Classical taste considered more attuned to Washington's character, were forwarded to the Association, and demands for an open competition were widely voiced. Discord almost killed the project then, but in 1847 the Association capitulated and set an open competition. Pollard resubmitted his opus, but the jury cautiously elected to approve Minard Lafever's colossal Egyptian obelisk. This in its turn remained unrealized, for with national attention focused on Robert Mills's monument (also an obelisk) for the Capital, the New York project lost impetus and was in due course forgotten.

James Dakin designed many of the outstanding antebellum buildings in New Orleans, most of them in a restrained Greek Revival mode. A few, however, notably St. Patrick's Church, he rendered in the Gothic style he had mastered during his association with Town and Davis. When it was decided to move the capitol from New Orleans to Baton Rouge, Dakin quickly seized the opportunity to obtain the prestigious commission for the new statehouse. He rapidly produced and submitted a well-conceived and polished design before anyone else had given the matter much consideration. The capitol commission was somewhat taken aback by the departure from the Classical tradition for state capitols represented in his Gothic proposal, but he justified the wisdom of his unconventional approach:

Design for a projected Washington Monument, New York, 1843. (New-York Historical Society)

> I have used the Castellated Gothic style of Architecture in the Design because it is quite as appropriate as any other Style or Mode of building and because no style or order of architecture can be employed which would give suitable character to a Building with so little cost as the Castellated Gothic.
>
> Should a Design be adopted on the Grecian or Roman Order of Architecture, we should accomplish only what would unavoidably appear to be a mere copy of some other Edifice already erected and often repeated in every city and town in the country. Those orders have been so much employed for many years past that it is almost impossible to start an original conception with them.

He obviously chose the Gothic style in no Romantic spirit; he was simply bored with Greek Revival and advanced the always popular plea of economy to justify a change in mood. The propriety of the style was not in question; he sought only for a practical and interesting solution. In this case he may have been influenced by Sir Charles Barry's Gothic Houses of Parliament then rising beside the Thames.

Completed in 1849, Dakin's capitol did not lack for critics, many of whom saw the building as a symbol of the oppression of the Dark Ages as opposed to the Hellenic democracy implicit in the Greek Revival, but general opinion was favorable. The *New Orleans Daily Delta* reported that the building exhibited "a variety and uniformity exquisitely picturesque and subservient alike to utility and ornament," whatever this may mean. Much of the effectiveness of the ornament, as well as the speed and economy of the construction, was due to the extensive use of cast iron. The building has had a checkered career. A fire in 1862, when it was a Union garrison, left only the blackened brick walls standing—a genuine, if modern, Gothic ruin which was neglected until funds were appropriated in 1880 to restore it as the capitol. William A. Freret, the architect in charge, was largely faithful to Dakin's design but elaborated upon it to the extent of inserting a great cast-iron spiral stair and rotunda, lit by a sizable glass monitor on the roof of the central block. He also raised the wings one story and added intricate iron turrets atop the main towers and slender bartizan towers at the corners of the center wings, both of which proved unpopular and were later removed. The executive suites were furnished with pieces originally ordered for Maximilian of Mexico, who was executed before they could be delivered to him. In 1932 Huey Long's skyscraper statehouse was completed, and the old capitol, having undergone several restorations, now serves as a museum and state office building.

Old Louisiana State Capitol, Baton Rouge, 1847–49, 1880–82.
Photographed ca. 1900. "Sir Walter Scott is probably responsible for
the Capitol building, for it is not conceivable that this little sham
castle would have been built if he had not run the people mad, a
couple of generations ago, with his Medieval romances.
The South has not yet recovered from the debilitating effects
of his books."—Mark Twain

IRON WORKS

*Townsend Monument,
Laurel Hill Cemetery, Philadelphia*

MID-NINETEENTH-CENTURY architects and engineers quickly learned that cast iron lent itself well to Gothic ornamentation and that a rich effect could be achieved with a minimum of expense and labor. This adaptability of material resulted in the appearance of Medieval mannerisms in unexpected places. Although cast iron was employed for the complete range of historical styles during the period, it seemed particularly well suited to the complex geometry and naturalistic detailing of the Gothic. It also answered the demands of an impatient country, for the growing cities and towns could not wait for stonecutters and artisans to painstakingly ornament the great quantities of buildings going up. By the use of cast iron a building could acquire "architecture" as quickly as the pieces could be bolted together.

R. A. Smith's 1852 guide to Philadelphia's Laurel Hill Cemetery, laid out by the fashionable necropolitan architect, John Notman, described the cast-iron monument to Samuel Townsend as the "first of that material erected in the United States," noting that it was similar to England's "far-famed Waltham Cross." (Waltham Cross is one of the Eleanor Crosses, a series of Medieval monuments erected at the places where the body of Queen Eleanor rested each night on its last journey from Lincoln to London in 1290. Mostly in the form of elaborate Gothic pinnacles, they provided design inspiration for numerous Victorian grave markers.)

The harsh outlines of industrial buildings were particularly susceptible of amelioration by means of cast-iron Gothic detailing. The smokestack that is the functional as well as visual focal point of the Central of Georgia Railway Shop is surrounded at its base by a polygonal cast-iron tank decorated with Gothic blind arcading and quatrefoil panels. The iron was cast by the Savannah foundry of William and David Rose, afterward famous as manufacturers of armor for Confederate ironclads. The Medieval theme is continued in the smokestack's brick base, which features a machicolated cornice above an arcaded foundation containing the workers' privies.

Cast-iron bridges with Gothic decoration are not unusual in Europe, especially in England, but are comparatively uncommon in the United States. Among the rare examples in this country was the Chestnut Street Bridge over the Schuylkill in downtown Philadelphia. Engineered by Strickland Kneass, the bridge was considered one of the handsomest in the city. Attenuated Gothic forms provided an appropriate type of enrichment for the wiry iron structural members. The spandrels were in the form of a tapered two-tiered Gothic arcade, and the sides of the soffit were ornamented by a series of quatrefoils. The structure was removed in 1958, an unfortunate loss.

The splendid tomb of James Monroe, the focal point of John Notman's romantically landscaped Hollywood Cemetery in Richmond, is a tour de force of both Gothic Revival architecture and craftsmanship in cast iron. The monument consists of a relatively simple stone sarcophagus, enclosed by an elaborate iron screen surmounted by an ogee dome with openwork tracery. The scheme recalls

Left, smokestack,
Central of Georgia Railway Shop,
Savannah, ca. 1850

Right, Chestnut Street Bridge,
Philadelphia, 1861–66

that of Henry VII's tomb in Westminster Abbey, also enclosed by a metal screen but lacking a dome. It was cast by Wood and Perot of Philadelphia to the design of Alfred Lybrock, a Richmond architect–engineer. President Monroe's body was moved to this final resting place upon the centennial of his birth in 1858.

Although cast-iron facades were extremely popular in the mid-nineteenth century, most were in the Italian Renaissance style; Gothic iron fronts are a great rarity. The former Bishop's House in Portland, Oregon, is a notable example. It was probably designed by P. Heurn of San Francisco, the architect of the Portland Cathedral. The audience hall was located behind the large traceried window on the third story. Sold by the Church in the 1890s, the building has since had a colorful succession of tenants. It was first the headquarters of a Chinese tong, later it became a speakeasy, and it later housed the offices of an architectural club.

Left, tomb of James Monroe, Hollywood Cemetery, Richmond, 1858

Right, Bishop's House, Portland, Oregon, 1879

Lenox Library, Princeton Theological Seminary. Photographed ca. 1870.

ANTEBELLUM COLLEGIATE

Left, Dwight Hall, Yale University, New Haven, 1842–46. (Harper's New Monthly Magazine, June 1858)

Right, Observatory, U. S. Military Academy, West Point, New York, 1841. (Harper's New Monthly Magazine, June 1856)

THE GOTHIC STYLE, although its possibilities for collegiate design had been demonstrated with the schemes for New York University and the Virginia Military Institute (qq.v.), was slow to take hold in academe. The Classical connotations of the Greek Revival were better suited to popular concepts of the collegiate purpose, and in the case of older schools the Grecian style blended pleasantly with earlier Colonial and Federal structures. Perhaps the strongest point in favor of Greek Revival was its basic simplicity (often reduced to absolute austerity for large dormitories), which made it more economical than the necessarily elaborate Gothic. The Gothic style, then, if found at all on an antebellum campus, was usually restricted to one or two isolated buildings, a chapel or perhaps a library. An early example was Gore Hall, the 1838 Harvard library designed by Richard Bond. This relatively uninspired building, vaguely

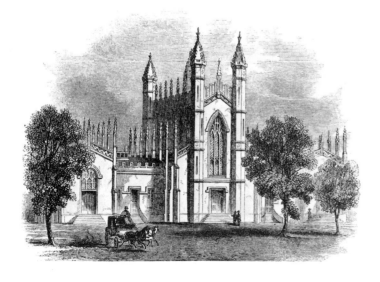

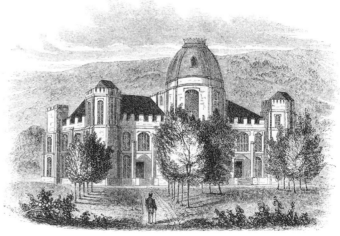

Old Main, Knox College,
Galesburg, Illinois, 1857

based on King's College Chapel, Cambridge, was taken down in 1913 to make way for Horace Trumbauer's Widener Library. At Princeton, one of the earliest Gothic Revival buildings was the Lenox Library, erected in 1842 for the Theological Seminary; this restrained, handsomely proportioned structure was demolished in 1955. In 1842–46 Yale built a Gothic library, Dwight Hall, which now serves as a chapel and meeting place. Also an adaptation of King's Chapel, it is one of the more elegant Gothic college buildings of the period. It was designed by Henry Austin, an architect formerly associated with Town and Davis, who opened a New Haven office in 1839. Although it now blends with the Ruskinian and twentieth-century Collegiate Gothic buildings surrounding it, it must originally have been a sharp contrast to the plain Colonial dormitories.

The United States Military Academy, later to become as much a showcase of all types of Gothic Revival buildings as Yale or Princeton, first received a Gothic accent in its observatory. Originally described as "English Tudor," it was completed in 1841 to the designs of the Academy's Superintendent, Maj. Richard Delafield, who decked it out in corner towers, crenelations, and even a buttressed dome. It was razed in 1961, and a new library erected on the site.

The mild resistance to the Gothic style displayed by established Eastern institutions was less apparent in some of the newer colleges farther west. In nearly all cases use of the style was restricted to one large building rather than an entire complex, but the Gothic touch gave these schools a much-needed look of permanence and prosperity. In 1857, only twenty years after its founding, Knox College in Galesburg, Illinois, erected a typical Gothic "main building." Designed and built by one Charles Ulricson of Peoria, the building's facade displays a somewhat stiff symmetry in contrast to the more informal massing then coming into vogue. It was chosen as the location for one of the Lincoln–Douglas debates in 1858.

Laurel Hill Cemetery chapel, Philadelphia, ca. 1837.
Detail from a gouache by Zeno A. Schindler.
(Museum of Fine Arts, Boston, Karolik Collection)

MORTUARY CHAPELS

By the middle of the nineteenth century, city churchyards and burial grounds were rapidly filling up. The large public cemeteries which succeeded them were of necessity somewhat removed from the towns they served, and the need for an appropriate shelter for services conveniently close to the gravesite gave rise to a new architectural form—the mortuary chapel. Elaborate Gothic creations, designed to satisfy Victorian fascination with the accoutrements of death, became the focal point of the many romantically landscaped cemeteries established in the middle years of the century. Like the architectural follies that often accented English gardens, these mortuary chapels had a more exotic flavor than would ordinarily have been tolerated in domestic, civil, or even denominational church

Bigelow Chapel,
Mount Auburn Cemetery,
Cambridge, 1843, 1858

buildings. The Edinburgh-trained Scot, John Notman (1810–65), who came to the United States in the early 1830s, created two important prototypes when he laid out Philadelphia's Laurel Hill Cemetery and designed its chapel. He specialized in cemetery design based on the eighteenth-century English school of natural landscaping. The Laurel Hill chapel, since destroyed, was an adaptation in miniature of an English collegiate one.

The Bigelow Chapel at Mount Auburn Cemetery, Cambridge, with its rather heavy pinnacles, was designed in 1843 by Dr. Jacob Bigelow, a professor at Harvard Medical School, who established the cemetery. Somewhat in advance of his time in hygienics, Bigelow founded the large cemetery on the edge of the city as an alternative to the already overcrowded Boston graveyards; he deplored the thought of additional burials in a city that still drew much of its water supply from individual wells. When the chapel's granite began to disintegrate in 1858, the building was dismantled and completely rebuilt.

The Gothic mortuary chapel crowning the central knoll of Greenmont Cemetery, Baltimore, is perhaps the most imposing of all the mid-nineteenth-century examples we have. Designed by John Niernsee and John Crawford Nielson, it is an octagonal structure with a central spire supported by flying buttresses; its total height is 102 feet. On an expanded scale it recalls the Medieval English market crosses in Salisbury and Chichester. The details are carefully carved in brown sandstone and accurately follow Medieval examples shown in the illustrations of such works as Pugin's. Still in use, the chapel's lofty interior retains its cast-iron Gothic catafalque.

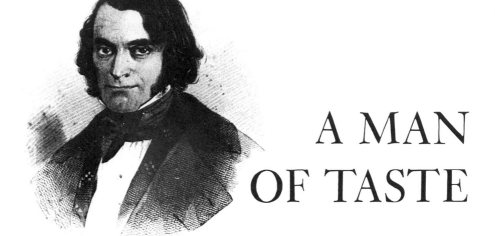

A. J. Downing. (Treatise on Landscape Gardening, *1856*)

A MAN
OF TASTE

ANDREW JACKSON DOWNING (1815–52) was, as a young but perceptive horticulturist, much disturbed by the state of America's domestic architecture. He looked about him and saw country houses thoughtlessly plunked down without regard to their relationship to the character of the surrounding landscape. He saw the affluent endeavoring to cram all the functions of modern domesticity within the confines of a Greek temple, while humbler folk were regimented into an endless and uninspired series of little white clapboard boxes with green shutters. The efforts of the more architecturally imaginative to bring a little romance into their style of living by building mock-Medieval castles of wood and plaster appeared to Downing pathetic and ridiculous. Although his first interest was in plants and landscaping, his distress at the lack of harmony between contemporary architecture and its natural surroundings forced him into his role as one of our major architectural critics and theorists.

His first book, *A Treatise on the Theory and Practice of Landscape Gardening, Adapted to North America* (1841), sought to define the properties of more tasteful rural architecture. He noted that by achieving picturesque forms through the use of porches, verandas, gables, chimneys, and so on, a house could be given "some reasonable connexion, or to be in perfect keeping with surrounding nature." In this and successive books he discussed how the Greek, Roman, Tuscan, Gothic, Swiss, and Rhenish styles, and their innumerable offshoots, might be modified and landscaped to bring them into harmony with American life and topography. He listed the merits of every mode, but his writings fail to disguise his bias for the Gothic. His own house, overlooking his beloved Hudson River, was a comfortable Tudor Gothic villa, built largely to his own design. To Downing the Gothic—Castellated, Tudor, or "Old English"—was the foundation of the Romantic school; diametrically opposed to the Greek or Roman Classical schools, it was far better suited to the Picturesque mood in landscape gardening which he championed so vigorously.

Downing was careful not to give blanket approval to anything that happened to have pointed arches and battlements. Much of his architectural criticism in fact was directed against what he considered the cheapness and inaccuracy of flimsy Carpenters Gothic. He deplored its tacked-together pinnacles and nailed-on towers, declaring: "There is a glaring want of truthfulness sometimes practised in this country by ignorant builders, that deserves condemnation at all times. This is seen in the attempt to express a style of architecture, which demands massiveness, weight, and solidity, in a material that possesses none of the qualities. We could point to two or three of these imitations of Gothic castles, with towers and battlements built of wood. Nothing could be more paltry and contemptible. The sugar castles of confectioners and pastry-cooks are far more admirable as works of art."

He felt that the style he termed Castellated was, in general, impractical. In his opinion, few Americans had sufficient means to build a proper castellated dwelling of brick or stone, and, should they do so, were not very likely to place it in an appropriately wild and Romantic setting. Since castles were originally intended for defense he concluded that to build one in the midst of level fields "would immediately be felt to be bad taste." He favored the Tudor style as the best form of Gothic for dwellings, especially for "villas" or large country houses. When acceptably built of stone or brick, the Tudor was "the most convenient, and comfortable, and decidedly the most picturesque and striking style, for country residences of a superior class."

Downing's residence at Newburgh, New York. (Treatise on Landscape Gardening)

Downing was not totally opposed to the use of wood in Gothic structures; he simply felt that certain expressions of the style precluded its use. He approved of wood for "cottages"—small single-family houses which he defined as occupied by "industrious and intelligent mechanics and working men, the bone and sinew of the land." Such Gothic cottages should not be watered-down versions of castles or Tudor mansions, but should follow the pattern of the vernacular rural Gothic or "Old English" Medieval house, which made generous use of wood in both structural elements and ornament. Adapted to American conditions, such cottages might have either stuccoed or board walls, and would be characterized by large roof areas and steeply pointed gables ornamented with finials and carved vergeboards (or bargeboards), a prime distinguishing feature of the late Medieval houses he admired.

Downing was one of the first Americans to make a clear distinction between domestic and ecclesiastical Gothic. In his *Treatise on Landscape Gardening* he decried the absurdity of building a miniature cathedral for a dwelling, and described how the English rural Gothic cottage, with its bay windows, diamond panes, fancy chimneys, and ornamented gables, could be made into a "perfect gem of a country residence." But he was quick to caution against overelaboration and short-cut workmanship. Too many gables could give a cottage a "cocked-hat" appearance, and vergeboards sawn from thin planks would impart a " 'ginger-bread' look which degrades, rather than elevates, the beauty of the cottage."

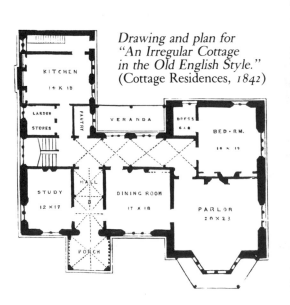

Drawing and plan for "An Irregular Cottage in the Old English Style." (Cottage Residences, *1842*)

In order to illustrate what he felt to be correct architectural taste, Downing, himself not an architect, collected favorite schemes from such noted practitioners as A. J. Davis, Richard Upjohn, and Gervase Wheeler, and published these examples not only in the *Treatise*, where they are little analyzed, but in two major collections: *Cottage Residences* (1842) and *The Architecture of Country Houses* (1850). In these volumes he included both plans and elevations, together with exhaustive descriptions of the houses illustrated and a good deal of practical information on their design and construction. Here Davis, whose taste coincided with Downing's, was of great assistance. These books were all immensely popular and ran through many editions. Downing's pungent, well-reasoned didacticism and attractive illustrations struck a sympathetic chord among laymen and professionals alike; the demand for houses in his version of the Gothic style spread rapidly, along with his enlightened principles of house design, which discarded the uncompromising format of the Greek Revival in favor of Romantic styles with more open and flexible floor plans. A pleasant asymmetry gained acceptance for its Romantic flavor and its adaptability to more functional and interesting interiors. Projections allowing for more windows and more light, and verandas to shade walls and provide outdoor shelter, were important features.

The success of Downing's books spawned many imitations; his practical, appealing approach proved a marketable commodity. After his example, through the 1860s the country was deluged by pattern-books containing designs for

Above, design for a cottage in the "light rural Gothic style suitable for the small farmer or the more liberal cottager." (Allen, Rural Architecture, 1852)

Below, porch detail. (Cottage Residences)

97

ornamental villas, cottages, outbuildings, farmhouses, churches, and public buildings, in every style touched upon by Downing. Among the more popular and influential of these books were William Ranlett's *The Architect* (1847), Lewis F. Allen's *Rural Architecture* (1852), Samuel Sloan's *The Model Architect* (1852), and Gervase Wheeler's *Rural Homes* (1853).

Downing unfortunately did not live to see the full flowering of his endeavors for he was drowned at the age of thirty-seven when the Hudson River steamer on which he was traveling caught fire and sank. Two years earlier he had contemplated giving up his nursery and landscaping business and formally taking up the profession of architecture. He hoped to form a partnership with Davis, but the scheme did not mature. However, on a trip to England in 1850, he met Calvert Vaux (1824–92), a young architect and landscapist well versed in Gothic design. The two became friends, and Vaux moved to America where he set up a firm with Downing which lasted until the latter's untimely decease. Vaux carried on the practice in the Downing tradition and became a most successful architect. He even produced a pattern-book of his own designs, *Villas and Cottages* (1857), which became the textbook for the architecture of the Hudson Valley. In his preface Vaux paid tribute to his former partner and assessed Downing's influence as a tastemaker: "He has set his mark fairly and broadly on the spirit of his age, and it is to be hoped that the love for grace and beauty that he so vigorously aroused in America will in future be always advancing."

Design for a gable of a Gothic cottage. (Sloan, The Model Architect, *1852)*

Fort Dalles, The Dalles, Oregon, ca. 1857. The surgeon's quarters, adapted from a design for "a symmetrical bracketed cottage," by Downing, 1853.

A satire on the vicissitudes attendant upon the creator of a Carpenters Gothic residence—the opening of a long set of verses by James Russell Lowell entitled The Unhappy Lot of Mr. Nott—*appeared in* Graham's Magazine *for April 1851. It so amused Downing that he included it in* Rural Essays *under the title "The Rural Cot of Mr. Nott." It was "too good to be lost sight of," he wrote, adding that a thought or two upon its moral "will help us all most essentially in this, our experimental art of architecture."*

My worthy friend, A. Gordon Knott,
  From business snug withdrawn,
Was much contented with a lot
That would contain a Tudor cot
'Twixt twelve feet square of garden-plot,
  And twelve feet more of lawn.

He had laid business on the shelf
  To give his taste expansion,
And, since no man, retired with pelf,
  The building mania can shun,
Knott, being middle-aged himself,
  Resolved to build (unhappy elf!)
  A mediæval mansion.

He called an architect in counsel;
  "I want," said he, "a—you know what,
  (You are a builder, I am Knott,)
  A thing complete from chimney-pot
Down to the very grounsel;
  Here's a half-acre of good land;
  Just have it nicely mapped and planned
And make your workmen drive on;
  Meadow there is, and upland too,
  And I should like a water-view,
D' you think you could contrive one?

(Perhaps the pump and trough would do,
If painted a judicious blue?)
The woodland I've attended to;"
[He meant three pines stuck up askew,
Two dead ones and a live one.]
  "A pocket-full of rocks 't would take
To build a house of freestone,
But then it is not hard to make
What nowadays is *the* stone;
  The cunning painter in a trice
  Your house's outside petrifies,
  And people think it very gneiss
Without inquiring deeper;
  My money never shall be thrown
  Away on such a deal of stone,
When stone of deal is cheaper."
And so the greenest of antiques
  Was reared for Knott to dwell in:
The architect worked hard for weeks
In venting all his private peaks
Upon the roof, whose crop of leaks
  Had satisfied Fluellen;
Whatever anybody had
Out of the common, good or bad,
  Knott had it all worked well in;
A donjon keep, where clothes might dry,
A porter's lodge that was a sty,

A campanile slim and high,
  Too small to hang a bell in;
All up and down and here and there,
With Lord-knows-whats of round and square
Stuck on at random everywhere,—
It was a house to make one stare,
  All corners and all gables;
Like dogs let loose upon a bear,
Ten emulous styles *staboyed* with care,
  The whole among them seemed to tear,
And all the oddities to spare
  Were set upon the stables.

Knott was delighted with a pile
Approved by fashion's leaders:
(Only he made the builder smile,
By asking every little while,
Why that was called the Two-door style,
  Which certainly had *three* doors?)
Yet better for this luckless man
If he had put a downright ban
Upon the thing *in limine*;
For, though to quit affairs his plan,
Ere many days, poor Knott began
Perforce accepting draughts, that ran
  All ways—except up chimney;
The house, though painted stone to mock,
With nice white lines round every block,
  Some trepidation stood in,

When tempests (with petrific shock,
So to speak,) made it really rock,
  Though not a whit less wooden;
And painted stone, howe'er well done,
Will not take in the prodigal sun
Whose beams are never quite at one
  With our terrestrial lumber;
So the wood shrank around the knots,
And gaped in disconcerting spots,
And there were lots of dots and rots
  And crannies without number,
Wherethrough, as you may well presume,
The wind, like water through a flume,
  Came rushing in ecstatic,
Leaving, in all three floors, no room
  That was not a rheumatic;
And, what with points and squares and rounds
  Grown shaky on their poises,
The house at nights was full of pounds,
Thumps, bumps, creaks, scratchings, raps—till—
  "Zounds!"
Cried Knott, "this goes beyond all bounds;
I do not deal in tongues and sounds,
Nor have I let my house and grounds
  To a family of Noyeses!"

COTTAGE RESIDENCES

Vergeboard. (The Architecture
of Country Houses, *1850)*

THE INFLUENCE OF Downing, Vaux, and their fellow producers of pattern-books may been seen all over the country. Many of the designs illustrated in their works are for wooden cottages which fall into the category of Carpenters Gothic. Often highly ornamental, they are, however, considerably more refined than the early versions of the style—the "gingerbread" houses denigrated by Downing.

Although generally unrecognized, the Gothic cottage is as much an American architectural institution as the log cabin, the saltbox, or the ranch house, and like

Ashcroft, Geneva, New York, 1862.
A contemporary photograph.
(Miss Sylvia Dakin Collection)

them embraces a considerable diversity within a loose generic definition. The word cottage may be applied to such an impressive residence as Ashcroft, in Geneva, New York, which was designed, along with its gardens and outbuildings, by Calvert Vaux himself, as well as to an anonymous millhand's dwelling in a factory town. The Gothic cottage was originally developed to harmonize with the unspoiled natural grandeur of the Hudson Valley, but it was shortly translated to quite different surroundings. For example, in 1851, Gen. Mariano Guadelupe Vallejo, a leading figure in the establishment of California as the thirty-first state, put up a pure Yankee Gothic cottage at Lachryma Montis, his ranch north of San Francisco. Its irregular plan, vergeboards, and pointed windows would fit comfortably into a New York State village. Settlers and fortune seekers in the fast-growing Golden State were eager to spend their new wealth on the latest fashions, but in their homes they wished also to recall the East they had left behind. The Gothic cottage, satisfying both requirements, soon became a familiar sight; in fact, the demand exceeded the available supply of local builders, and a number of these houses were prefabricated on the Atlantic coast and shipped round the Horn to California.

Lachryma Montis, Sonoma, California, ca. 1851. Lithograph after a painting by S. W. Shaw. (California State Library)

Left, Neff Cottage, Gambier, Ohio, ca. 1860

Right, Mosswood, Oakland, California, 1864

Gothic cottages have sheltered many an American celebrity besides General Vallejo. The co-inventor of the tintype photographic process, Peter Neff, built an unusually polished wooden example in Gambier, Ohio. The sophisticated handling of the details suggests that the house was designed by a professional architect, probably William Tinsley, an Irishman at that time working for Kenyon College. Remarkably, the elaborate woodwork is all hand-finished rather than sawn, and would for that reason alone have won Downing's approval. Among other well-known figures who were born or lived in Gothic cottages are Amelia Earhart, Gen. John J. Pershing, and Ring Lardner. Rest Cottage, a board-and-batten structure typical of the Midwest in the 1860s, was long the home of Frances E. Willard, first dean of women at Northwestern University, and founder of the Women's Christian Temperance Union. The house is now maintained by the W.C.T.U. as a memorial to its pioneering leader.

One of the purest examples of the Gothic cottage in the San Francisco Bay Area is in Oakland, where S. H. Williams designed Mosswood for J. Mora Moss. The house is an exercise in sober boldness, lacking any of the frippery commonly associated with cottages; the central pavilion is firmly supported on its brackets, and the dormers firmly attached to the eaves. The solidity of the composition is underscored by the deep shadows cast by the California sunshine.

Wesleyan Grove, a Methodist camp meeting ground at Oak Bluffs on Martha's Vineyard, must be the greatest concentration of Gothic cottages in the world. They were built, mostly in the late 1860s, to take the place of the tents usually associated with such camps. Although their builders gave imagination free rein in these fanciful creations, almost every one had a Gothic theme. An 1868

Above, Rest Cottage, Evanston, Illinois, 1865

Below, Oak Bluffs, Martha's Vineyard, Massachusetts. Three cottages in Wesleyan Grove, ca. 1866.

description summarizes their character: "Over the front door there is generally a balcony. The high-peaked roofs, the balconies, the door and window frames, are all decorated with scroll-work; stained glass, silver doorplates, hanging lanterns, and other luxuries are beheld at every turn." By the close of the century, all the tents had been replaced and there were more than a thousand cottages packed onto the narrow lots. Of these, perhaps three hundred remain; those illustrated here only hint at their variety.

No Gothic cottage is better known than the simple board-and-batten house in the background of Grant Wood's painting *American Gothic.* In 1929 Wood, holding an art festival in Eldon, Iowa, noticed the house and found time to sketch its facade. The painting was executed the following year. The couple in the foreground are not Mr. and Mrs. Gideon Jones, who lived in the house at the time, but the artist's sister Nan Wood Graham, and his dentist, Dr. B. H. McKeeby, both of whom posed elsewhere. (Mrs. Graham saw the house for the first time in 1973.) The cottage was erected in 1881–82 for Charles Dibble, and is attributed to Messrs. Busey and Herald, local carpenters.

American Gothic *by Grant Wood, 1930. (Art Institute of Chicago)*

Dibble House, Eldon, Iowa, 1881–82

CREATURE COMFORTS

Design for a bed. (Arnot, Gothic Architecture Applied to Modern Residences, *1849)*

GOTHIC IN THE nineteenth century was by no means confined to exteriors. Rooms were decorated and furnished in Gothic motifs, and designers produced a full range of suitable domestic appurtenances, including furniture, clocks, lamps, stoves, and tableware. It became possible to achieve total Gothic. The epitome of this development may be seen in the A. J. Davis dining room at Lyndhurst (q.v.), where nothing is left un-gothicized. Most of these rooms were Tudor in feeling, as exemplified in an illustration from Downing of Kenwood, the Joel Rathbone house just south of Albany. Ceilings rarely rose to a pointed arch, being mostly flat and ornamented with ribs, but pointed arches appeared almost anywhere else they could be worked in—on windows, doorcases, mantels, and furnishings. Kenwood is now an interdenominational school; the house has disappeared, but some outbuildings and the gatehouse remain.

Many houses followed a Gothic theme throughout, and in those that did not it was fashionable to have at least one Gothic room. This was very often a library, where dark woods and narrow windows might conjure up an ambience of scholarly isolation from the modern world. The first floor of the octagonal "tower of books" at Rokeby, the Astor house on the Hudson River, is a fine example of such a library. The room is finished with rich wood-grained surfaces, and the bookcases and openings form a continuous "arcade" with a result that is both cozy and impressive, a happy combination for any bookroom. It was added to the house at some time after John Jacob Astor gave Rokeby to his son William for a wedding present. The exact date and the architect remain unknown, for William Astor burned all his papers before he died.

A number of cabinetmaking firms developed suitably gothicized lines of furniture and fittings. In New York, Joseph Meeks and Sons, Burns and Trainque, and Alexander Roux were among the leaders, and in Philadelphia, Crawford and Riddle, Michel Bouvier, and George J. Hinkels sold tables, chairs,

Armchair in the style of Meeks, ca. 1850.
(Tucker Herrin Hill Collection)

Design for a staircase.
(*Arnot, Gothic Architecture*
Applied to Modern Residences)

"Drawing Room at
Kenwood, Gothic Style."
Table at center now in
Lee B. Anderson Collection.
(*The Architecture of Country Houses*)

and case pieces in the pointed style. Baltimore also had its share of craftsmen producing what one contemporary critic ungraciously described as "instruments of torture." These artisans created unmistakably Gothic objects with considerable imagination and ingenuity, uninhibited by the paucity of Medieval models. Traceried windows inspired chairbacks, tables were supported on clustered columns, and bookcases, secretaries, and other case pieces were embellished with such architectural ornaments as columns, crenelations, and quatrefoils.

In 1842 the English-born cabinetmaker Robert Conner published his *Cabinet Maker's Assistant* in New York. It was the first work in America to be devoted to Gothic furniture, but there were more to follow, and Downing took up the subject in *The Architecture of Country Houses*. Noting that much Gothic furniture was to be criticized because "it is too elaborately Gothic—with the same high-pointed arches, crockets, and carving usually seen in the front of some cathedral," he tried to show that furniture could be so felicitously designed "as to unite a simple and chaste Gothic style with forms adapted to and expressive of our modern life."

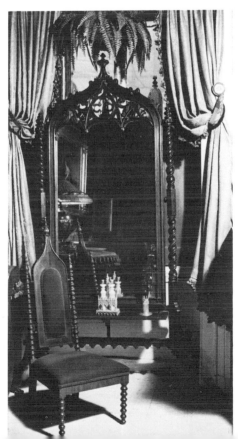

Left, Rokeby, Red Hook, New York, 1815. The octagonal library, added in the mid-19th century.

Right, a Gothic ensemble. The mirror is part of a set made by Michel Bouvier (1792–1874) and owned by Prince Joseph Bonaparte. The child's chair is by George J. Hinkels. (Lee B. Anderson Collection)

Design for a rustic privy and toolshed.
(Vaux, Villas and Cottages, 1864)

PAVILIONS & OUTBUILDINGS

THE "TRUE PRINCIPLES of Gothic architecture," as advocated by Pugin, failed to dampen the free use of the style for secondary and ornamental structures. Constrained by Pugin and Downing, the Victorian American may have felt obliged to exercise some restraint in the design of his residence proper, but he could and did give fancy free rein in subsidiary buildings. Gothic, particularly playful Carpenters Gothic, lent itself readily to the purpose; as in the eighteenth century, it was one of several styles adapted to provide light-hearted garden accents, cheerfully lacking in religious or philosophical overtones.

Since the days of William Penn, Philadelphia families have had country places on the Delaware; it was a pleasant thoroughfare. "The Delaware River, above Philadelphia, still flows through a landscape too level for beauty, but it is rendered interesting by a succession of gentlemen's seats, which, if less elaborately finished in architecture, and garden grounds, than the lovely villas on the Thames, are still beautiful objects to gaze upon as you float rapidly past on the broad silvery stream that washes their lawns." So wrote Frances Trollope in her 1832 *Domestic Manners of the Americans*. This painting of unknown provenance (it was discovered at a church auction), shows a developing country seat, with a Gothic summer house at the water's edge that has some of the exotic flavor of the houseboats of Kashmir. The exact location is not known; it is believed that once it graced the western shore of the Delaware somewhere between Andalusia, above Philadelphia, and Bristol, where the river bank is lower and bulkheaded in places, as shown in the painting. A fitting companion to the Grotto at Andalusia, the summer house and its estate were doubtless swamped in the advancing tide of the industrial age.

Andalusia, the Biddle family seat, is a multistructured complex. The main house, transformed into a Neo-Greek temple by Thomas U. Walter in 1834–36, is the focus of various cottages, farm buildings, and the dairy, besides the two-story

Left, Andalusia, Pennsylvania, the Grotto

Right, design for a cattleshed
in the guise of a ruin. (Decorations for
Parks and Gardens, ca. 1804)

Below, American landscape by an unknown artist.
(Edward Swain III Collection)

Right, Old Homestead, Aberdeen, Mississippi, ca. 1852, carriage house showing icicle-like bargeboards and lattice tracery

Below left, gazebo, 31 Meeting Street, Charleston, before 1848

Below right, design for a "flower stand." (Sloan, The Model Architect, 1852)

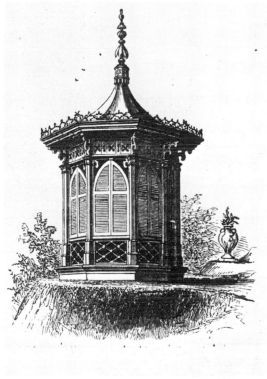

Classical Revival "Billiard Room" by the river, and the Gothic folly in the form of a ruined grotto which stands at the other end of the lawn. The Billiard Room was intended as a sanctum for the gentlemen, the Grotto as a place for the ladies to pause for rest or shelter in the course of a stroll. A drawing, unfortunately undated, in Walter's own hand shows the original conception as a larger structure, featuring a corner tower, which was not built. Even without it, the Grotto is a rare surviving example of a "new ruin," reminiscent of earlier English landscapes wherein bloomed arbors, temples, and columns as well as grottoes.

A particularly charming southern example of Gothic secondary buildings is the gazebo in the large garden of the house at 31 Meeting Street in Charleston. The main feature of the space, it is built in the full exuberance of Carpenters Gothic and is placed on axis with the main entrance of the house. Framed in crepe myrtle, it serves to soften the severe line of the adjacent house wall, as well as to provide a summer shelter. The grilles on either side of the center doors are bowed in; their projecting sills may have supported statues or urns in their more glamorous youth.

Left, guard house, Fairmount Park, Philadelphia, ca. 1850

Right, design for a suburban summer house. (George E. and F. W. Woodward, Country Homes, 1866)

GOTHIC ITALIAN-STYLE

FROM THE END of the Civil War to the close of the nineteenth century, American Gothic architecture was largely shaped not by any architect but by the works of the English critic John Ruskin (1819–1900), whose immensely influential books on art and architecture were even more widely read in this country than in England. His theories gave rise to the new expression of Gothic that is today referred to as High Victorian, a term that describes most of our major Gothic works from this period. His two chief architectural treatises, *The Seven Lamps of Architecture* (1849) and *The Stones of Venice* (1851), were published simultaneously in New York and London and ran through repeated editions until after his death. Ruskin wrote so much and said so much during his long career that it is difficult to sum up his attitudes toward buildings old or new. Much of his writing is contradictory (some, in fact, is nonsense), but his enthusiasm combined with a gift for forceful expression served to make him one of the most popular writers of his time. Today his ideas seem outmoded and his approach to new buildings irrelevant, but his works remain Victorian classics of the history of taste.

Ruskin was born of cultured and well-to-do parents who early reached the conclusion that they were blessed with a gifted child. They devoted their lives to fostering his genius and shielding him from any coarse influence that might affect the purity of his outlook. He was educated at home up to university level; when he went up to Oxford his mother went with him. His parents were the strictest of Protestants, and for the fifty-two years that Ruskin lived with them his Sundays were spent in religious contemplation and Bible study. The elder Ruskin was a prosperous sherry merchant, whose son often accompanied him on business trips; the boy was sixteen when he first visited Venice, the Medieval architecture of which he lived to make the admiration of the English-speaking world, and a good bit of the rest of it as well.

To the end Ruskin never wavered in his belief that Gothic was a virtuous style, fit to inspire modern work. Like Pugin, he believed strongly in the moral and ethical nature of architecture, and judged old buildings by the virtue of their builders. But despite these points of basic agreement, he felt little admiration or affection for Pugin. Their fundamental differences were at least as strong as their sympathies, and the greatest divergence was undoubtedly in matters of religion. The staunchly Protestant Ruskin was not at all attracted by the mystical and symbolic associations of the Gothic which were major factors in Pugin's conversion to Catholicism. Moreover, he felt a personal dislike for English Gothic ("wildness without invention, and exuberance without completion"), whereas Pugin devoted his life to promoting it.

It must be remembered that Pugin was an architect and Ruskin was not. Pugin thought in three-dimensional terms and could comprehend the interplay of spaces so evident in English Gothic. He could appreciate the beautiful logic of the Gothic structural systems, and the role of ornament in complementing the total composition. Ruskin, on the other hand, for all his profound appreciation of architecture, never really visualized the third dimension. A watercolorist, he saw buildings primarily as a series of planes, two-dimensional compositions susceptible of enrichment with colored masonry or ornamental accents. Perhaps the weakness of one eye affected his depth perception, so that he was unable to perceive architectural mass or volume. He was certainly unaffected by the spatial grandeur of English Gothic and dismissed it as a jumble of carving, "small pinnacles, and dots, and crockets, and twitched faces." Ruskin's concept of architecture as a series of patterned planes, and his love for clear and subtle coloring, combined to attract his fancy to the Gothic palazzi of Venice. As a Victorian moralist, he rationalized their beauty by assuming that they were built by virtuous men, although, in actual fact, the successful Venetian merchants for whom they were created were in all likelihood somewhat less virtuous than the ecclesiastical authors of the English Gothic churches for which he had so little use. His bias was confessed: "The Gothic of the Ducal Palace of Venice is in harmony with all that is grand in all the world: that of the North is in harmony with the grotesque Northern spirit only."

Ruskin's inspiring delineations and analyses of Medieval Venetian buildings form the body of *The Stones of Venice*, one of the greatest works of architectural appreciation ever written. It awakened Englishmen and Americans alike to the rich and delicate beauties of a type of Gothic hitherto largely ignored. One of the Venetian characteristics Ruskin stressed was the use of architectural coloring. He felt that a polychrome effect on a building should be achieved through the juxtaposition of differing masonries; paint or imitation materials were unethical, indeed, unthinkable: "the colors of architecture should be those of stones." He also emphasized the Italians' suave and restrained use of ornament as opposed to the overall deep-relief effect of Northern Gothic. "The Italians fearlessly left fallow large fields of uncarved surface, and concentrated the labour of the chisel in detached portions, in which the eye, being rather directed to them by their isolation than attracted by their salience, required perfect finish and pure design rather than force of shade or breadth of parts."

Ruskin advocated the Gothic as a suitable model for contemporary buildings, but there was a curious ambivalence in his feelings about Gothic Revival. He sang the praises of the Italian Gothic, especially the Venetian, for page after page, and the Mediterranean flavor of many a High Victorian Gothic work may be traced to his silvery descriptions, but he never actually recommended making modern copies of it. It was for him an aesthetic perfection, to be emulated rather than imitated. Reproductions of his beloved Venetian palazzi, set down in an alien context, could only be viewed as in bad taste. To his dying day he was distressed by the Italian Gothic banks, pubs, and shop fronts that sprang up all over late nineteenth-century England, and he blamed himself for their existence. This is perhaps why, in spite of his distaste for English Medieval architecture, he did not hesitate to declare Gothic of the English Decorated style to be the most appropriate model for the Gothic Revival, promoting his *bête noir* in an effort to preserve the purity of his *beau ideal*, but the effort was unavailing. Ruskin's writings made the Italian Gothic so appealing that architects on both sides of the Atlantic hastened to capitalize on it, the more so as the fresh impulse came just when the Gothic Revival stood badly in need of renewed inspiration. The English Gothic vein was nearly worked out; here was a new source and a new approach.

Americans, always taken with a new idea, greeted Ruskin's writings with enthusiasm and took to building in Italian Gothic even more readily than did the English. Lacking a Gothic of their own, Americans were not troubled, as were some Englishmen, by the substitution of an alien for a national style. In the hands of gifted architects Ruskin's writings prompted the creation of a series of boldly handsome buildings that have only lately been properly valued for their conceptual grandeur, richness of material, and quality of craftsmanship. Interpreted by less able practitioners, however, his precepts inspired some grim and ponderous piles of masonry upon which much of the blame must rest for the long period of prejudice against late Victorian architecture. Successful or not, these polychromed Italianate buildings form a major facet of America's High Victorian Gothic and are classified as Ruskinian in acknowledgment of the famous critic who would doubtless have found fault with them all.

The National Academy of Design (1862–65), by Peter Bonnett Wight, is a prime example (and a very early one) of the inspiration derived from Ruskin by American architects and designers. Here the very arbiters of national taste saw fit to house themselves in a scaled-down adaptation of the Doges' Palace in Venice. Wight followed Ruskinian principles to the extent of using native plants as models for the ornamentation. The structure was acclaimed in *The New Art*, the journal of the Association for the Advancement of Truth in Art, a group dedicated to

Top, National Academy of Design, New York, 1862–65

Above, Our Lady of Lourdes, New York, 1902–04.
Many of the architectural features of the lower story
of the National Academy of Design were salvaged
and incorporated into this church,
which still stands at 467 West 142 Street.

Left, Chapel Hall, Gallaudet College,
Washington, D.C., 1867

promoting Ruskin's ideals, but ultimately even Ruskin and Wight could not prevail against commercialism; the exquisite *palazzetta* was pulled down in 1899.

Chapel Hall, the architectural focal point of Gallaudet College, the only institution of higher learning for the deaf in the United States, is another relatively early example of Ruskinian Gothic. It is part of the original complex designed by Frederick C. Withers, who formed a partnership with Vaux in 1866. Here he produced a distinguished example of polychromed Italian Gothic in the Ruskinian manner, complete with an American eagle over the center arch to signify the school's national importance. Vaux and Withers went on to create many more buildings in the High Victorian Gothic, of which the Jefferson Market Courthouse (1875) in New York is one of the most famous.

Gothic was the basis for the stylistic vocabulary of Frank Furness (1839–1912), one of the most original architectural geniuses this country has produced. In his highly personal oeuvre he combined Ruskin's concepts of ornamentation with the rationalistic credo of the French theorist Viollet-le-Duc that engineering is the essence of Gothic. Furness acquired his eclectic and somewhat formal approach to design at the outset of his career, when drafting for Richard Morris Hunt (q.v.). The Pennsylvania Academy of the Fine Arts, designed in partnership with George W. Hewitt, was his first major commission, and it gained him national recognition. Its straightforward three-part facade and mansard roofs illustrate the disciplined influence of Hunt and the École des Beaux-Arts. The polychromed Gothic detailing and naturalistic carvings follow Ruskinian principles of ornamentation, and the teachings of Viollet-le-Duc are evident in the decorative metal monitors (since removed) in the wings, and in the exposed I-beams, iron Gothic columns, and metal skylights of the interior. The effect of this emphasis on the synthesis of structure and ornament may be traced in the work of Louis Sullivan, who was in his turn a draftsman for Furness. The Gothic of Furness's later

Pennsylvania Academy of the Fine Arts, Philadelphia, 1871–76

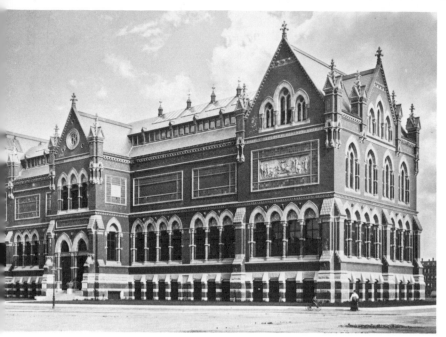

buildings received an even more personalized treatment; toward the close of his career his details had evolved into abstract compositions bearing little relation to Medieval precedent.

Traditionally, public buildings in Boston have conformed to the latest architectural fashions. It is not at all surprising that the Museum of Fine Arts, a major civic monument, was the last word in Ruskinian High Victorian Gothic upon its completion in 1878. Richly decked in Italian details, the self-confident structure was one of the first of several architectural landmarks to be built on Copley Square. John H. Sturgis, of the firm of Sturgis and Brigham, was the chief architect. Born a British subject in the Philippines and trained in England, Sturgis was one of Boston's leading architects in the post-Civil War era, and was a strong advocate of the use of terra cotta, an economical and durable material highly suitable for crisp Gothic details. The museum was a fitting container for its artistic treasures, but it survived hardly more than a quarter of a century, for in 1908 the exhibits were moved to the present huge Neoclassical structure, and the old museum was taken down to make way for the Copley Plaza Hotel.

Memorial Hall at nearby Harvard University ranks among the most ambitious expressions of Ruskinian influence in the country, and the fact that its architecture owes little to Italian precedent would probably have earned Ruskin's approval. It was conceived by his friend Charles Eliot Norton as a memorial to Harvard's Civil War dead, and represents one of the few instances in which the conservative university "went overboard," for even Harvard was not exempt from the Victorian conviction that depth of feeling is directly proportionate to the size of the monument. The building was an architectural success. Not only did it provide a handsome and proper symbol of Harvard's sorrow; it housed much-needed facilities. The "nave," under a great open-timber ceiling, contains a large convocation hall that also served as the main university dining room. The Memorial Hall itself, with its decorated tablets and inscriptions, occupies a vast lateral passage beneath the tower, while the "apse" provided space for an ingeniously designed theater. The clock in the soaring tower was the university's chief timepiece until 1956, when the whole upper portion of the airy structure

Left, Old Museum of Fine Arts, Boston, 1872–78

Right, Memorial Hall, Harvard University, Cambridge, 1870–78

117

was burned because of a carelessly handled blowtorch. The building was the product of the Boston firm of Ware and Van Brunt. William Robert Ware organized the M.I.T. architectural school, first in the United States, and founded the Columbia University School of Architecture. Henry Van Brunt's scholarly activities included translating Viollet-le-Duc's *Entretiens sur l'architecture* under the title *Discourses on Architecture* (1875).

The complex history of Nott Memorial Hall, Union College, is illustrative of the warm welcome accorded polychromed Italian Gothic on American college campuses in the 1870s. Ever since the original building scheme for the school had been laid out by J. J. Ramée in 1813, Union College had striven to complete his plan by erecting his intended architectural focal point—a domed rotunda. In 1858 foundations were at last laid for an Italianate building adapted from Ramée's design by Edward Tuckerman Potter, who had trained under Upjohn and was the grandson of Union's president, Eliphalet Nott. Lack of funds halted construction at that point, and nothing further was attempted until around 1870, when a more mature Potter scrapped his original plans in favor of a far bolder and more fashionable design, a colorful adaptation of the Gothic baptistery in Pisa. That this conception was quite alien to Ramée's flanking Neoclassical buildings did not appear to trouble the trustees; construction began in 1872, and by 1876 was completed save for the clerestory windows. The sixteen-sided building, erected on the 1858 foundations, is named in honor of President Nott. Its richly decorated walls demonstrated Potter's sure grasp of Gothic design, but today this polychromed masonry is totally covered by massive creeper. In 1902 the clerestory windows were installed and the building converted into a library under the supervison of Edward Potter's brother, William Appleton Potter, architect of the Chancellor Green Library at Princeton. The library has since been relocated and the structure currently serves as a theater.

William Potter's exquisite five-part Chancellor Green Library adheres as closely to Ruskin's theories and principles as his brother's building at Union College. Resembling no Gothic structure of the past, it is one of the most original compositions of American High Victorian Gothic. Its varied materials form rich polychromed surfaces, and the skillfully handled details emphasize a lively geometry. The interior is even more unrestrained, but handled with equal self-assurance. Few greater tributes to Ruskin's singular genius exist on either side of the Atlantic. By 1896 the building was no longer adequate to house the university library and Potter designed a new adjacent structure, in English Collegiate Gothic. Now stripped of many of its interior appointments, Potter's masterpiece receives rough-and-tumble use as a student center and eating place.

A product of Edwardian wealth and optimism, Fenway Court, Boston's Venetian "palazzo turned inside-out" is the creation of that imaginative patron of the arts, Isabella Stewart Gardner, who acquired her appreciation of Venetian Gothic from Charles Eliot Norton. The works of art purchased by the Gardners in Venice during the 1890s inspired them to create a private museum in which to exhibit their acquisitions. John L. Gardner felt that their Beacon Street house was too small for this purpose, and tried to persuade his wife that they should erect a new building in Frederick Law Olmsted's newly created park on the Fenway. Mrs. Gardner balked at so remote an address, but when her husband died

Chancellor Green Library, Princeton University, New Jersey, 1873. Photograph before 1896.

suddenly in 1898 she decided to carry out his wishes. She commissioned Willard T. Sears to design a museum on the site, but dominated the planning herself, employing her favorite Venetian Gothic style. The building's character was in a sense predetermined in Venice in 1897, when the Gardners acquired eight balustrades from the Ca' d'Oro, which had been replaced because of their weathered condition. This purchase led to the collecting of other architectural fragments—window frames, balconies, capitals, and the like—with which the Gardners planned to embellish their new museum. Sears convinced Mrs. Gardner that these items could not withstand the extremes of Boston winters, so she determined to concentrate the building's architectural elaboration on a magnificent glass-roofed interior court. The exterior is little more than a buff brick box without a hint of the grandeur within—a wholly intentional dramatic contrast.

A festive Venetian palazzo "right-side-out" is the "Pink Palace," standing on Meridian Hill, Washington, D.C. It was designed by George Oakley Totten, Jr., for Mrs. John B. Henderson, who lived nearby in now-demolished Boundary Castle, one of Washington's largest and grimmest Victorian mansions; she commissioned the Pink Palace and several other large houses along Sixteenth Street in the hope of creating an Embassy Row. Totten's choice of the Venetian Gothic mode may have resulted from a lingering Ruskinian influence, but he had studied at the École des Beaux-Arts, where small attempt was made to attach a Ruskinian morality to past architectural styles; the design is probably rather an outgrowth of Edwardian eclecticism. Mrs. Henderson's hopes to the contrary, the mansion never became an embassy. It was for a time the home of Mrs. Marshall Field, and now houses the offices of the Inter-American Defense Board.

LATER
VICTORIAN
CHURCHES

*The Little Brown Church in the Vale,
near Nashua, Iowa, 1864, needlepoint*

IN THE POST-CIVIL War years new influences bombarded American church architecture. The doctrines of Pugin and the Ecclesiologists still carried weight, and Ruskinian precepts were steadily gaining ground. Architects of European training introduced continental Gothic forms; native designers, caught up in the current of eclecticism, produced increasingly individualized interpretations of the Gothic; and local contractors and country carpenters, often freely combining elements from pattern-books, created spirited church buildings, plain or fancy according to demand. Romanesque Revival (as popularized by H. H. Richardson), Italianate, Second Empire, and Queen Anne modes were also often employed, so that the ecclesiastical architecture of the last quarter of the century is as richly various as the domestic.

In spite of the growing popularity of other styles, the Gothic continued to hold its own in church design, since the dwindling demand for it in residential work (see p. 139) seems not to have much affected ecclesiastical projects. No doubt its identification with historic religiosity was a factor in maintaining its vigor; in any case, we have a great number of late nineteenth-century Gothic churches. They wear many guises: great soot-encrusted hulks looming over rows of industrial houses, cheery white-washed meetinghouses dappled in the sunshine of small villages, red brick "Big Baptist" edifices standing importantly on downtown streets, and little wooden country churches along the roadside. The American Gothic church fitted itself to every taste, faith, and location, drawing on a common architectural vocabulary to produce manifold echoes of the Medieval heritage.

Hardly distinguishable from a myriad similar buildings, one modest country church is known to thousands through an old familiar song. Dr. William S. Pitts of Wisconsin, journeying by stagecoach through Iowa around 1860, noticed a beautiful grove which struck him as the perfect setting for a church. Back at home, he wrote a nostalgic ditty about the church as he had envisioned it, and to his amazement, on passing the same spot five years later, he saw his daydream in reality. Even the color was right, because, as the pastor explained, brown paint was cheaper than white. Pitts made another journey, with music in hand, and the song that is now a part of our folk memory was sung for the first time by the congregation of "The Little Brown Church in the Vale." The plain wooden building, carrying a steep gable roof behind a square tower, is typical of modest churches and chapels of the time. The only distinctively Gothic elements are the tower and the pointed arches of the openings, but they suffice to give the unpretentious structure a quietly religious air.

The much-photographed 1829 Federal church facing the Litchfield, Connecticut, Green today—the admiration of tourists and a source of pride to the community—lost both its site and consecrated character for more than fifty years as a result of Victorian ecclesiastical taste. It had gone quite out of style when Henry Ward Beecher wrote of it: "There was not a single line suggesting taste or beauty." By that time the Episcopal and Catholic Litchfield churches had achieved buildings in the most up-to-date Carpenters Gothic (neither of which survive), so that when expensive repairs to the fabric of the Congregational structure became necessary, the church was moved off the site and replaced with a contemporary one. In March 1877 *Harper's New Monthly Magazine* reported, "The church . . . diverted from sacred uses, is now a public hall, and the present Congregational Church, a beautiful structure, but unfortunately of wood, is the growth of the present decade." (The wooden construction deplored by *Harper's* was specified by the major contributor to the building fund.) It was replete with turrets and pinnacles, its polychromed roof was topped with iron crestings, and a corner tower, a favorite device of the day, dominated the composition. Thriftily, the congregation mainly reserved the use of flush boarding to the facade, employing utilitarian clapboard elsewhere. The meeting room was unencumbered by supporting piers. Lit by side windows and high dormers, it was painted and stenciled and the pulpit backed by a great pointed arch beneath the painted admonition "Worship the Lord in the Beauty of Holiness." By 1929 public taste had swung full circle; the old-fashioned Victorian building was pulled down to make way for the restoration of the present church.

The extremes to which Carpenters Gothic could be carried and its persistence in rural areas are both illustrated in the Waddell Memorial Presbyterian Church in country Virginia. A positive forest of spires sprouts from the nave, transepts, and vestry of the board-and-batten structure. None of the architectural motifs are carved or finished with any particularity; milled boards were reduced to the desired shape by hand sawing, and nailed together to form the details. The church was designed by J. B. Danforth, an amateur architect from Richmond, whose drawings are still in the possession of the congregation.

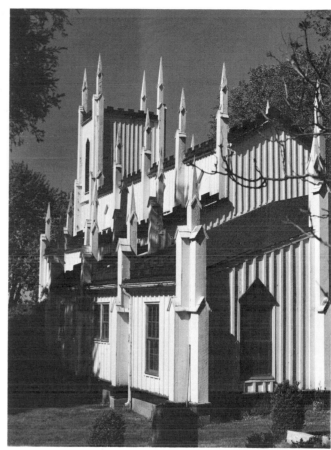

Isolated communities did not always settle for naive wooden churches. The solid masonry Victorian Gothic of St. Mary's in the Mountains is a startling contrast to the flimsy ghost-town architecture of Virginia City, Nevada, that surrounds it. It is much in the mode of contemporary urban Catholic churches; the machicolations lining the eaves, the three portals, and the spire rising from the center bay of the facade are characteristic features. The building looks quite capable of withstanding the "zephyr" that swept away one of its frame predecessors. Virginia City is situated on Mount Davidson, where the silver deposits of the Comstock Lode (which helped pay for, among other things, a good part of San Francisco, the Civil War debt, and the laying of the Atlantic cable) were discovered. Even St. Mary's bell was cast of Comstock silver.

Virginia City was not the only western community to boast an imposing religious edifice. When the Mormons migrated to Utah they took with them a predilection for the exotic and celestial in religious architecture, seeking a "heavenly" aspect in their houses of worship, as they raised the Kingdom of Zion in the Utah desert. Following the precedent of the Kirtland Temple (q.v.), the settlers borrowed freely from a variety of historic styles, combining various elements in singular, often bold creations. Many of the nineteenth-century tabernacles which dominate the communities surrounding Salt Lake City make use of a Gothic vocabulary, and Box Elder is a striking instance. Brigham Young

Left, First Congregational Church, Litchfield, Connecticut, 1873

Right, Waddell Memorial Presbyterian Church, Rapidan, Virginia, 1874

St. Mary's in the Mountains,
Virginia City, Nevada, 1873–77

selected the site, on the crest of an alluvial hill in the center of Brigham City, in 1865, but work on the tabernacle progressed slowly. Stone for the walls was hauled in over the next eleven years, and the actual construction continued for fourteen years more. The designer was probably Truman O. Angell, Jr., or his more noted father, best remembered as the designer of the Temple in Salt Lake City, a building that defies stylistic categorization. Gutted by fire only six years after it was finished, Box Elder was rebuilt within its massive walls in 1897, when sixteen brick buttresses with gablets and pinnacles were attached to the sides and the pointed domed tower was added at the front. It is still the spiritual and architectural focus of Brigham City.

Isaac M. Wise Temple is a Gothic church with Moorish icing, designed by James Keys Wilson (1828–94), who had worked for Renwick and was best known for his residential work in the Gothic Revival style. The combination of Gothic and Moorish Revival modes which Wilson, working closely with Rabbi Isaac Mayer Wise, produced became, for many years, the architectural signature of Reformed Judaism, in the history of which Rabbi Wise is a towering figure. The three-bay facade with high, accented nave and deeply recessed doors is that of a Christian basilica; the rose windows above the west door and over the altar at the east end of the nave strengthen this impression, but the points of the arches are not emphasized, the twin towers crowning the facade resemble minarets, and the low-relief ornamentation is Byzantine. Wise himself described the building as "an Alhambra temple with slender pillars and thirteen domes"—one for each of the thirteen attributes of God (Exodus 34). The domes are shallow and visible only from within the building. This curious amalgam of styles owes much to the Romantic movement in Western Europe, combined with a desire to reflect the Near Eastern origins of the Jewish people; the result is both impressive and sophisticated.

The Chapel of St. Peter and St. Paul, called the first "true collegiate chapel" in the United States, has been a prototype for many of its academic fellows. The original chapel at St. Paul's School, the first Episcopal preparatory school in New England, is a small Romanesque building which by 1886 was outgrown. The newer structure was designed by Henry Vaughan (1845–1917), a transplanted Englishman who had studied with George Frederick Bodley, called by the Archbishop of Canterbury "the foremost Gothic architect in England." His training was in the pure fourteenth-century English Gothic, and his chapel exemplifies that style. Ralph Adams Cram (q.v.) has described the building as

Left, Box Elder Tabernacle, Brigham City, Utah, 1876–90, 1897

Right, Isaac M. Wise Temple, Cincinnati, 1863–65

"the beginning of the Gothic Revival—or rather initiation—in America." Like its English models, it has a long narrow nave with choir seating, and a wooden barrel-vault ceiling. Vaughan also designed the oak benches and the fittings of the sanctuary. When consecrated in 1888, the chapel had no tower and only one stained-glass window; Vaughan added the tower and reredos in 1894. The photograph here antedates work done by Goodhue and by Cram and Ferguson in the 1920s; in 1928 the sanctuary was moved eastward, two additional bays added to the chancel, and the choir room extended.

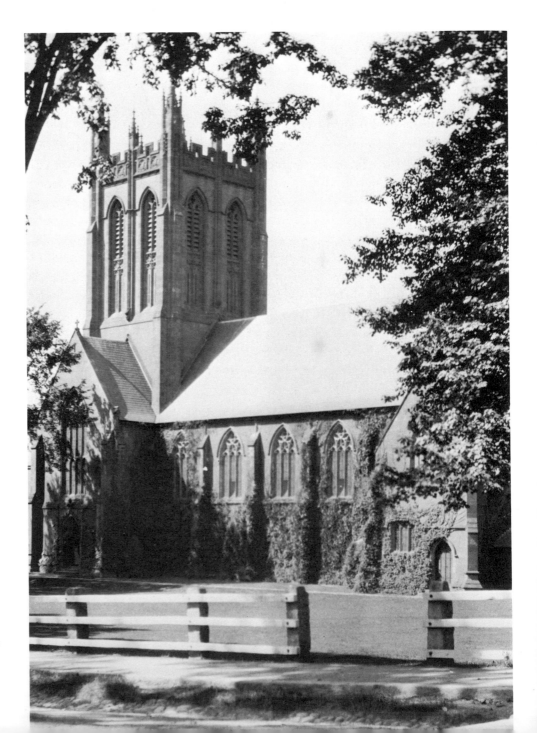

Chapel of St. Peter and St. Paul, St. Paul's School, Concord, New Hampshire, begun in 1886. An 1896 photograph.

GRAVE MANNERS

Dexter Mausoleum, Spring Hill Cemetery, Cincinnati, 1869. (Howe's Historical Collections of Ohio, 1889–91)

AN INDEX OF American prosperity in the latter half of the nineteenth century is the increasing elaboration of our cemeteries and tombs. It was a time when grief was expressed in architecture of considerable monumentality, and death became the foundation of a viable industry, involving cemetery companies, funeral homes, and monument manufacturers. The large urban cemetery, managed as a private corporation, evolved into an American institution. A community in microcosm, it was endowed with administrative building, real estate office, street and water systems, open spaces, and chapel; it had its good addresses and back alleys, and even a dump. On a Sunday afternoon one might stroll down its landscaped avenues and admire the solemn memorials of its first families just as one might promenade the boulevards of the city past the mansions of the prosperous living.

Death need mean no loss of dignity for a person of means. For the individual who required a lasting tribute in proportion to his testamentary dispositions, a stone mausoleum—the grander the better—was most suitable. Indeed, it became a major status symbol, a way of showing that one's pocketbook was so ample that one could afford to take a bit along. Religious overtones made the Gothic style de rigueur for a majority of these miniature temples of the departed, and many architects of the period produced distinguished examples. James K. Dexter's tomb in Cincinnati approaches the ultimate in private mausoleums. A scaled-down version of Paris's Sainte-Chapelle, this Flamboyant resting place was designed by James K. Wilson (q.v.), one of the city's leading Victorian architects and designer of many of its Gothic buildings. Wilson achieved his mastery of the mode through training under James Renwick, Jr.

One notable necropolis is Crown Hill Cemetery in Indianapolis, designed in Olmsted's Romantic landscape tradition. Buried there beneath monuments befitting their stature are Benjamin Harrison, Booth Tarkington, and Eli Lilly. Separating this community of eternal peace from the world of those yet to cross

127

over is an earthly version of the pearly gates, a stone Gothic archway recalling the three-portal entrances of French cathedrals. This classic of Victorian cemetery architecture was erected in 1885 to the designs of Adolph Scherrer, a native of Switzerland whose talents were cultivated in the Fine Arts Academy of Vienna. Though less showy, it follows the precedent set by the main gateway of Brooklyn's Greenwood Cemetery, designed in 1861 by Richard Upjohn in partnership with his son, Richard Mitchell Upjohn.

In far-off Hawaii the use of the Gothic for so symbolic a structure as a royal mausoleum shows the extent to which the island kingdom had succumbed to western influence by the 1870s. Because he wished to lie near his mother, King Lunalilo refused to be buried in the royal family's new mausoleum in Nuuanu Valley, and willed that a special tomb be built for himself in Honolulu. The architect for the royal commission was Robert Lishman, an Englishman who came to Hawaii in 1871. With an unquestioning faith in the aesthetic values of his own country and generation, Lishman provided the Pacific monarch with a mausoleum in respectable High Victorian Gothic. Because of the paucity of good local stone Lishman was forced to resort to a relatively new material, concrete block.

*Crown Hill Cemetery gates,
Indianapolis, 1885*

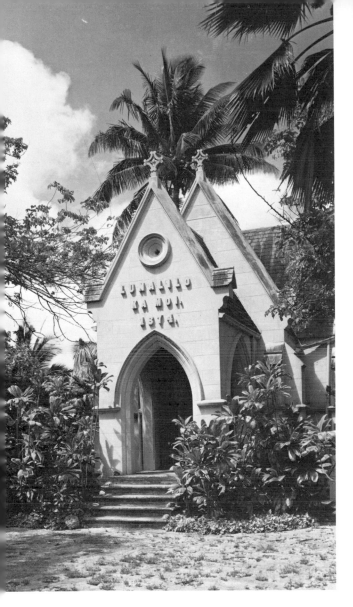

Impressive as other examples may be, the premier essay in American Gothic funeral architecture is unquestionably the great monument and tomb of President James A. Garfield. The Garfield National Monument Association was established in 1882 in Cleveland, Garfield's former home, to undertake the erection of a suitable memorial to the fallen leader. An open competition for the design was won by George Keller, a Hartford architect who specialized in elaborate monuments, including the Gothic Memorial Arch on the Connecticut capitol grounds. Keller was assisted in the project by John S. Chapple of London, who supervised much of the mosaic and stained-glass work. The plans called for a 150-foot tower of Ohio sandstone so sited on an eminence in Cleveland's Lakeview Cemetery that it could be seen for miles. In contrast to the rather forbidding exterior, the interior is a masterpiece of rich Victorian Gothic decoration. The walls of glittering mosaic and polished granite form a resplendent backdrop for the gleaming white marble statue of the twentieth president. Few chief executives, kings, or emperors have had their mortal remains so extravagantly sheltered.

Left, King Lunalilo Mausoleum, Honolulu, 1874-75

Right, Garfield Monument, Lakeview Cemetery, Cleveland, completed in 1890

FIRE & WATER

Standpipe, Fairmount Park,
Philadelphia, ca. 1855.
(Free Library of Philadelphia)

COMPARING THE PUBLIC works of the last century with those of today, one becomes conscious of how alien these Victorian expressions of civic pride are to us. In an age of complexity we demand simplicity; but in the earlier era, when cities were young and raw and generally monotonous, the demand for picturesque relief, preferably of an historic flavor, was at its greatest. Conspicuous public facilities, such as fire-houses and water towers, provided an excellent opportunity for the creation of imaginative architectural eyecatchers. The standpipe shown here is an early example of Gothic motifs used to embellish a public utility; it stood in Fairmount Park until 1932. Designed by the engineering firm of Brickinbine and Trotter, the pipe was supported in a buttressed masonry base and encircled by a winding stair that ascended to an observation platform, making a joy of a necessity. Whether the figure of Washington ever did grace the top is not certain.

When the City of Baltimore took over the management and facilities of the independent fire companies, one of its requirements for each engine house was a watchtower. Accordingly the city received a Florentine Gothic touch when, in 1853, a tower inspired by Giotto's Campanile for the Florence Cathedral was added, by the firm of Reasin and Wetherald, to Engine House 6. Its striking qualities are emphasized by its strategic location at the junction of two major downtown streets.

Much admired as an historic landmark, Chicago's famous water tower, designed by the prolific William W. Boyington, nevertheless has not always received favorable criticism. It has been accused of being more suitable to a goldfish bowl, and Oscar Wilde, on a visit to Chicago in 1882, declared it "a castellated monstrosity with pepper boxes stuck all over it." The tower was one of the few buildings to survive the great fire of 1871. Its ebullience even exceeds that of the North Point Water Tower in Milwaukee, also shown here.

Although the Brooklyn Bridge is more famous as a marvel of engineering than as an architectural work, it is an important part of our Gothic heritage. Begun by John A. Roebling and completed by his son Washington, the bridge makes use of Gothic arches in its massive stone pylons more for structural reasons than from any desire for historicity. The slender pointed arches are a pleasing visual counterbalance to the horizontal sweep of the span and the cables. Pointed-arch cross-bracing appears on a number of modern steel-pylon suspension bridges, such

Left to right:
Engine House 6, Baltimore, 1853;
Chicago Water Tower, 1869;
North Point Water Tower,
Milwaukee, 1874

as the St. Johns Bridge in Portland, Oregon, giving them a perhaps fortuitous Gothic aspect.

Few American cities have produced buildings so picturesquely exuberant as San Francisco. The Gothic confection illustrated was built for Engine Company 15 in the period when fire companies vied with one another in putting up the most elaborate engine houses. Its Gothic "style" was merely a vehicle for ornateness and shows the High Victorian Gothic in its freest interpretation. The Victorian love for literal symbols is apparent; the pinnacles were in the form of fire hydrants and the center pinnacle crowned by a fireman's hat. A utilitarian feature, the hose-drying tower, was disguised in the Hansel-and-Gretel corner cupola. Unfortunately the building was destroyed in 1959.

Brooklyn Bridge,
New York, 1867–83

St. Johns Bridge,
Portland, Oregon,
dedicated 1931

Engine Company 15,
San Francisco, 1884

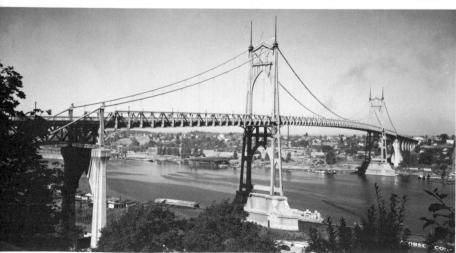

A DIGNITY
OF
APPEARANCE

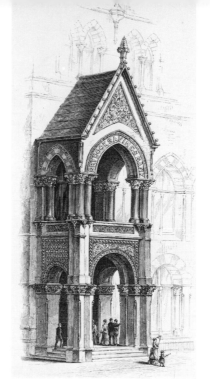

*Drydock Savings Bank, New York,
1870, by Leopold Eidlitz.
Demolished. (Art Journal, 1876)*

THE LATE CARROLL Meeks described the period of High Victorian Gothic as a "world of unabashed opulence and splendour, of rich color, of visible, unashamed evidence of material success and its concomitant belief in the increasing prosperity and irreversible progress of the civilized world" (*Arts in Virginia*, Spring 1962). The years between the Civil War and the First World War may not have been a golden age for humanitarians, but for architects things have rarely been better. The flood of immigration brought with it a bottomless cruse of cheap labor which included many skilled artisans: masons, stone carvers, carpenters, and plasterers, all trained in the artistic tradition of generations. Marbles and granites, exotic woods, gold leaf, copper and bronze, were easily come by for extravagant embellishment. A building came to be judged much on its size and commodious-ness, but also on the quality of its fabric and its beauty of ornament. Rich to an extent hitherto undreamed of, America yielded to the impulse to flaunt her new wealth. Industry and academe vied with one another in undertaking grandiose projects, and, as Meeks said, "every right-thinking person felt that public buildings must express in the most majestic way possible the power of government and that its representatives must be housed as splendidly as possible."

Many architects saw the Gothic as the only proper style for these prodigious commissions. Ruskin's oft-reissued books served to keep it in the vanguard of fashion, especially as his demands for truth in structure and fabric could now be met so readily and the inherent complexity of the style offered the maximum potential for elaboration. The long-favored English Gothic forms began to wane in popularity, and the Perpendicular and Tudor variants disappeared almost altogether from the repertoire. The majority of American High Victorian buildings, apart from certain churches, can hardly be said to display much fidelity to actual Medieval models. Like Downing's ornamental cottages, they were essentially modern structures designed to meet modern needs; their surface adornment was chiefly intended to ally them with great past traditions, and to endow them with the quality identified by Ruskin as "character."

Gothic's solid masonry and restless ornaments were applied, in one form or another, to large buildings of every purpose: city halls, courthouses, theaters, railroad stations, banks, colleges, and even a state capitol. Although English stylistic precedent was relied upon less and less, English Gothic Revival works continued to pave the way for United States counterparts. The Houses of Parliament made Gothic acceptable for legislative buildings, G. E. Street's Courts of Justice inspired judicial structures, American trustees hailed England's many new academic complexes, and Sir Gilbert Scott's extraordinary St. Pancras Station put notions in the heads of railroad presidents. American as well as English efforts in High Victorian Gothic have been condemned for vulgarity even as they have been admired for their dignity, but those that have survived the thoughtless destruction of recent years are worthy of preservation as unabashed declarations of the opulent materialism of a more confident age.

An exuberant example of High Victorian Gothic that stops just short of architectural absurdity is the massive Connecticut State Capitol. This Classical, five-part, domed building tricked out in Gothic finery is the magnum opus of Richard Upjohn's son, Richard Mitchell Upjohn (1827–1903). The gilded dome, its Renaissance drum encrusted with level upon level of Gothic details, represents the acme of the period's audacity; in no other era would an architect have dared such vigorous stylistic liberties. Henry-Russell Hitchcock condemned the capitol as "singularly vulgar" and "stylistically ambiguous," but nevertheless declared it to be the only major American public building in its mode with any pretension to

*Connecticut State Capitol,
Hartford, 1872–80*

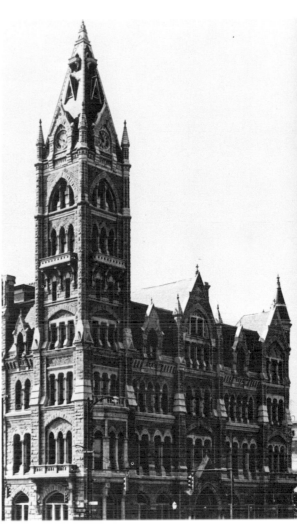

greatness or luxury of materials. The building is certainly vulnerable in its highly individual use of a Gothic vocabulary, but an impressive site, imposing scale, and lively outline combine to give it undeniable grandeur, and it must command admiration for the exquisite craftsmanship of its masonry. Within, it is a masterpiece of spatial design and Victorian decoration, displaying a richness of color and ornamentation that conceivably might even have gained Ruskin's approbation.

More restrained on the outside though no less noble within, is the Old Richmond City Hall, currently the temporary home of the Law Courts. Located in the heart of the city, immediately behind Jefferson's Classical capitol, the capacious gray pile is a granite synthesis of continental Gothic forms and late Victorian civic architecture. It was designed by the talented, although nearly forgotten, Elijah E. Myers (1833–1909) of Detroit, who was the architect of the state capitols of Colorado, Idaho, Michigan, and Texas, and of the territorial capitol of Utah (now the City and County Building of Salt Lake City). His career was crowned when he won the international design competition for the parliament buildings in Rio de Janeiro. Myers worked with agility in Classical as well as Gothic idioms, but his Gothic works appear the more distinguished. The Salt Lake City building and the now-vanished Grand Rapids City Hall, which resembled the Richmond edifice, both mined a bold and lively Gothic vein.

Myers's municipal structure provided psychological and aesthetic uplift to the former capitol of the South, graphically symbolizing recovery from the poverty and humiliations of Reconstruction, and its architecture is appropriately festive. The carefully articulated exterior preserves a ceremonious dignity (Myers held that in public buildings "a dignity of appearance is demanded"), but the interior is generous Victorian Gothic at its most brilliant. Offices and courtrooms surround a central four-story court bounded by a swirl of arches, columns, balustrades and chandeliers. The grand stair rises from the east end of the court, ascending in three broad flights to the topmost level. Richmond, used to the best, was once more able to command it; the building is a municipal palace.

Described in contemporary accounts as "Italianesque Gothic," the prodigious Cincinnati Music Hall is a theatrical amalgam of Gothic motifs, conforming to the Victorian thesis that the outside of a building should reflect the nature of the activities to take place within. It was designed by Samuel Hannaford, whose family had come from England and settled near Cincinnati. By the 1870s the city had become famous for music festivals and educational programs, but lacked a permanent facility for musical performances. In 1875 Reuben R. Springer, a local philanthropist, offered to pay half the cost of such a building, and active campaigning raised the other half; the Music Hall was completed three years later. The home of the Cincinnati Symphony Orchestra and Summer Opera, and the setting for many other programs, it is still the visual symbol of Cincinnati's flourishing musical tradition. The Brooklyn Academy of Music by Leopold Eidlitz (1860, destroyed in 1903), was another example of the association of the lively arts with Medieval modes. The Blue Grass Palace, built by the Blue Grass League in southern Iowa, carries the idea a step further to include a building intended as an agricultural exhibition hall; it was in part constructed of bluegrass

*Blue Grass Palace,
Creston, Iowa, 1889.
(The Illustrated West,
October 1891)*

hay and local grains and displayed a multiplicity of styles in keeping with its variety of material.

The most extraordinary design for a High Victorian Gothic complex in this country was never fully realized. When Trinity College sold to the city its original Hartford campus, where Richard M. Upjohn's capitol now stands, the trustees purchased a tract of land on a ridge overlooking the city, and sent President Abner Jackson to England to commission "a preliminary plan from any architect he might select." Jackson, on the advice of architectural historian John Henry Parker, selected William Burges, younger and less noted than Parker's other choice, Sir Gilbert Scott, but highly regarded as a practitioner in the Gothic style. Jackson then inspected various Gothic academic examples in Britain, and he was much struck with the appearance of Trinity College, Glenalmond, Scotland, a boys' school housed in a Victorian Gothic complex arranged around a large quadrangle, with a principal facade consisting of a three-story range or "long walk," picturesquely broken by gables, pavilions, and a central tower. Glenalmond became the basis of Jackson's concept of his own Trinity. He worked closely with Burges in preparing the plans, down to the last detail, and the collaboration produced a bold and ambitious four-quadrangle scheme with a "long walk" facade of over a thousand feet. This collegiate Kremlin incorporated a chapel, library, museum, dining hall, art building, theater, and observatory, together with dormitories and professors' apartments, all rendered in polylithic English High Victorian Gothic.

The enthusiastic trustees voted to begin construction in 1874. The Hartford architect F. H. Kimball was hired to supervise the building, and went to England to work with Burges on the preparation of working drawings, many of which are preserved at the college. Preliminary cost estimates soon reduced the projected four quadrangles to three. But President Jackson died just before the ground-breaking date, and his magnificent dream began to fade in the light of harsh realities. His successor, Thomas Ruggles Pynchon, rightly viewed the project as an enormous folly, certain to precipitate the College into bankruptcy; he courageously confined construction to only two buildings, Seabury and Jarvis Halls, which together comprise hardly more than a tenth of the original conception. They were completed in 1878, the only part of Burges's scheme ever realized, and at least form an impressive, if truncated, version of the "long walk" so dear to President Jackson.

Following the trend fostered by Trinity and the rugged buildings at Cornell University, solid Gothic "main buildings" became a distinguishing feature of many new institutions, particularly at land-grant colleges. Kirkland Hall, at Vanderbilt University, completed in 1875 to the designs of William C. Smith of Nashville, was a typical "old Main." With a bow to current fashion, Smith crowned the building with a mansard roof, a lack of architectural purity that did not escape remark. *Frank Leslie's Illustrated Weekly*, noted: "The style is Gothic of the thirteenth century except for the roof." (Twenty years later Smith further demonstrated his eclecticism by designing a replica of the Parthenon for the Tennessee Centennial Exposition.) Heavily damaged by a fire in 1906, Kirkland Hall was significantly restyled during restoration.

Right, Original four-quadrangle plan for Trinity College, Hartford, 1874. (Trinity College)

Left, Kirkland Hall, Vanderbilt University, Nashville, 1875

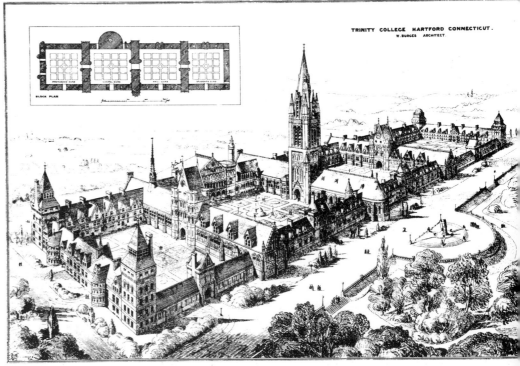

CHANGING TASTES

Porte cochere, Lindenwold Avenue, Ambler, Pennsylvania

AFTER NEARLY FIFTY years of ascendancy, in the 1870s and '80s the Gothic style in domestic architecture was quietly nudged aside by newer fashions. The cottage *ornée* and Tudor villa lost their cachet; the deep brackets of Florentine palazzi, the mansard roofs of Parisian *hôtels* came to represent the acme of success and advanced taste. A younger and self-confident generation of architects began to depart from strict historicism and became proficient in modern, more original modes, including Shingle Style, Stick Style, and Queen Anne. Gothic continued to hold its own for churches and institutions, but ever fewer full blown Gothic houses were commissioned; moreover, compared to lively earlier counterparts by Davis, Vaux, or Wheeler, they were somewhat gloomy affairs.

Ambler, Pennsylvania, more than makes its contribution to the numbers of these ponderous essays. Except for the town mansion, a huge, ill-defined castle, it was once a wholly Gothic enclave. It was designed and built to a semifeudal pattern by Richard Vanselous Mattison, asbestos tycoon, who created street after street of dwellings for his executive and other employees. Lindenwold Avenue, hard by the castle, was the most impressive address, with houses to match; the porte cochere shown here, with its machicolations surmounted by cast-iron crenelations, has its fellow at the other end of the street. Highland Avenue boasts less ostentatious residences for less exalted echelons, and the scale and decoration along each thoroughfare decrease with the position of its original tenants. Trinity Episcopal Church and Manse are the high point of this multiple exercise in dinosaur Gothic, and the rough-cut stone of which they are built serves to emphasize their grim and massive complexity.

The weighty Gothic mansion designed by George H. Smith to stand among the procession of magnates' houses on Euclid Avenue in Cleveland, was another typical example of these somewhat humorless late Victorian domiciles. Its Gothic encrustations, emphasized by an overly complex facade and a multiplicity of small

windows, gave the building the haunted-house look which unfortunately made Victorian a pejorative word in architecture for the first half of the twentieth century. Along with most of its proud neighbors, the mansion did not outlast the period of revulsion.

Happily, contemporary houses of Gothic persuasion did not all subscribe to these solemn, overbearing approaches. Architects employing the so-called Stick Style, which came to fruition in the 1870s, frequently relied on Gothic motifs to enliven their otherwise highly original works. As the name implies, Stick Style buildings are of wood, and their basic character is achieved through the lavish use of exposed timbers suggesting or actually serving as structural members. The style was largely an outgrowth of Downing's insistence on fidelity to material. He had maintained that wood should never be used in imitation of other materials in architecture, but only for forms adapted specifically to timber construction: vergeboards, roof trusses, siding, and so on. Downing's ideas were picked up and extrapolated upon by such other authors of pattern-books as Henry W. Cleaveland and Gervase Wheeler. By the 1870s the Stick Style had lost almost all relevance to historical modes, save for a vague vestigial resemblance to Tudor half-timbering. Some Stick Style builders, however, took their inspiration from the visible structural systems of the Gothic, and made use of stylized Gothic motifs in their ornamentation. Henry Austin, the architect of Villa Vista, charmingly incorporated pointed arches, gable ornaments, and other Gothic forms

140

into the two-level front porch and several gables. The porch is intended to look like an unencased unit of the overall framing system.

New architectural fashions may have supplanted the "pure" Gothic house throughout most of the country, but down in the bayous of Louisiana the outmoded cottages of Davis and Downing had still at least one loyal supporter. Mrs. John Dalton Shaffer, forced by delicate health to take a three-year rest cure in Europe, persuaded her husband to build, in her absence, a comfortable cottage on their plantation against her return. Shaffer engaged John Williams of New Orleans to design a house for a site selected by Mrs. Shaffer overlooking the bayou. The resulting twenty-one room "cottage" took the full three years to build (1897–1900). Tradition has it that the design was based on an English castle, but the sawn vergeboards, ornate veranda, and asymmetrical facade make the house essentially an expanded version of Downing's Gothic cottage. The fundamental difference between Ardoyne and its predecessors is in size. Downing's cottages were cozy, if not modest, but Ardoyne boasts an entrance hall seventy feet in length and has sixteen-foot ceilings. Mrs. Shaffer apparently approved of her cottage, for she lived in it for the rest of her life, and it is the home of her descendants today.

Left, Villa Vista, Stony Creek, Connecticut, 1878

Right, Ardoyne, Terrebone Parish, Louisiana, 1897–1900

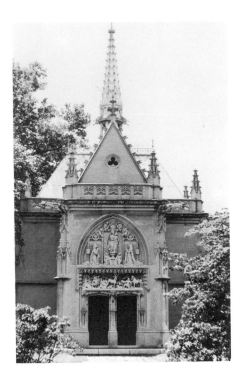

THE GILDED AGE

Belmont Mausoleum, Woodlawn Cemetery,
The Bronx, New York, 1909.
Designed by Hunt & Hunt, sons of R. M. Hunt.

THE LAST YEARS of Victoria's reign were marked in this country by the birth of a sort of colossus complex among those persons of large fortune then building residences. Apparently inexhaustible wealth, combined with the immigration that provided a seemingly equally inexhaustible supply of skilled workmen and knowledgeable servants, led to the construction of a number of great houses comparable in scale to the seats of European nobility and gentry. Nor were architects wanting to assist their clients in the realization of these weighty dreams of grandeur; Richard Morris Hunt, Stanford White, and George Browne Post were among those in the forefront. The lion's share of these behemoths have failed to survive the ever-shortening supply of great personal wealth and the virtual extinction of the professional servant class; those that remain are almost all preserved as museums, schools, or other public buildings. Many of them are splendidly uninhibited adaptations of the late Gothic chateaus of the time of Francis I, a style popularized principally by Hunt and eagerly seized upon by his fellow designers.

The majestic schemes of Richard Morris Hunt (1827–95) were in perfect accord with the aspirations of the rich and fashionable of his day. He had mastered French idioms while working in the Paris atelier of H. M. Lefuel, serving with him as inspector for the additions made to the Louvre in 1854. The first American to study his profession at the École des Beaux-Arts, he retained a predilection for the style of Francis I, but nevertheless drew for his effects on many periods and places. From the great French gates on Bellevue Avenue to the Chinese teahouse overhanging the Atlantic, the disparate details of Marble House and its estate reflect his eclectic inspiration. Marble House, like its fellows demurely called a cottage, cost William K. Vanderbilt $2,000,000 to build and $9,000,000 to furnish. The exterior is Louis XIV-Neoclassic, but the showpiece within is a Gothic room intended to display the Gavet collection of small Gothic objets d'art.

The original red damask of the walls above the carved wainscot, together with stained glass, polychromed ceiling, and great bronze chandeliers must all have contributed to the Gothic mood. The center of interest is the chimney breast, composed of crouching figures, standing figures, panels of domestic scenes, crenelations, and pinnacles—in short, the whole Gothic vocabulary. All the furniture was made for the room, and some of it has remained there through successive ownerships, to pass, with the estate, into the custody of the Preservation Society of Newport County.

Belcourt, also by Hunt, was designed almost simultaneously with Marble House. It was the Newport cottage of bachelor-sportsman Oliver H. P. Belmont, who afterward married Mrs. William Vanderbilt, the first woman elected to the American Institute of Architects. It is much in the style of a Louis XIII hunting lodge, combining residence and stables under a single roof. The stables are commodious and were splendidly maintained; it is said that the Belmont horses received a change of linen bedding thrice daily. The domestic quarters, not extensive by Newport standards, are augmented by a huge and impressive ballroom. In *The Architectural Heritage of Newport, Rhode Island*, Downing and Scully comment: "The interiors [at Belcourt] especially, and in particular the great ballroom with its castellated fireplace topped by sculptured figures leaning over the battlements, seem to reflect, through a wild and distorting lens, the whole vigorous and living stream of the mid-century Gothic Revival." Hunt actually used the Gothic idiom for interiors only rarely; this ballroom and the Gothic Room at Marble House are two of the few surviving examples.

William K. Vanderbilt's brother George, having chosen the mountains of North Carolina rather than the salt-splashed coast at Newport for his rural retreat, eventually acquired an estate of over 125,000 acres in the vicinity of Asheville. He

Left, Marble House, Newport, Rhode Island, 1892, the Gothic Room

Right, Belcourt, Newport, 1892, the ballroom

Biltmore House, Asheville, North Carolina, 1890–95

commissioned Hunt to design a suitable house. The original concept was repeatedly expanded, partly to accommodate the growing number of treasures brought from Europe by the owner, and partly to house under one roof most of the facilities necessary to make the establishment self-sufficient. The laundries, storerooms, and stables, the bowling alleys and the indoor pool, are all incorporated in the main house; there are 250 rooms in all, from the bedrooms for family, guests, and numberless servants to the banquet hall which measures 72 by 42 feet and has a 75-foot ceiling.

The completed exterior scheme was inspired by the chateaus of Chambord, Chenanceaux, and Blois. Late Gothic forms embellished with Renaissance ornamentation are the keynote of these transitional sixteenth-century creations, and decorative details from northern Italy applied to elaborate roofs of the feudal period intensify the late Gothic spirit of Biltmore House. Artisans were brought from all over the United States and from Europe to cut and fit the Indiana limestone of which the house is built, and to execute the elaborate carvings. Hunt did not live to attend the Christmas party in 1895 at which the mansion was formally opened, and two reception rooms were left unfinished. Biltmore House is now a house museum, owned by the family, and the farms and greenhouses are still in operation. In 1975, the two unfinished rooms are at last being completed.

The interior of Hearst Hall might be called the apotheosis of the pointed arch in domestic decoration; the vast room, created by Bernard Maybeck (1862–1957) for Phoebe Hearst, a patron of the University of California at Berkeley, was a reception hall where she could entertain the entire faculty at once. It was housed in a separate building, sheathed in redwood shingles and carrying a garden around its roof, and was originally connected to the Hearst residence by a footbridge. Maybeck was a creative and resourceful architect. Trained as a wood-carver, he had a special affinity for fine craftsmanship in wood, and during his years in California he developed a very personal architectural style in that material, which was compounded of more or less equal portions of Gothic, Japanese, Bungaloid, and Maybeck. Although Hearst Hall had slightly futuristic leanings, the room was dominated by its great Gothic arches, repeated and stressed wherever the eye might fall. After Mrs. Hearst's death the Hall building was moved to the university campus where it served as a women's gymnasium. It burned to the ground in 1922.

George Merritt not only doubled the size of the house at Lyndhurst (q.v.), he also erected an enormous greenhouse on the property. In addition to plants, the building housed service areas, bowling alleys, a gymnasium, and a billiard room. Jay Gould purchased the estate in 1880, seven years after Merritt's death, and began to reestablish the plant collection, but eight months later the greenhouse

Left, Hearst Hall, Berkeley, 1899. A contemporary photograph.

Right, the greenhouse at Lyndhurst, Tarrytown, New York, completed 1892, west entrance

and its contents burned. Gould immediately arranged for its replacement by the local firm of Lord & Burnham, fabricators, retaining the New York architectural firm of Pugin and Walter to introduce the Gothic details that tied the mammoth structure into the Lyndhurst scheme.

The new greenhouse was even larger than the old, which had been the biggest in the country, and was devoted entirely to plantings. It became famous for its palms and orchids, and for the fruit and flowers which supplied many neighboring institutions as well as the house. At this period the building was open to the public every day except Sundays, and it became a trendsetter, the forerunner of the great conservatories in Lincoln Park in Chicago, in the San Francisco Golden Gate Park, and in the New York Botanical Gardens. During the Second World War, maintenance began to present serious difficulties, and by the time Lyndhurst passed to the National Trust in 1966 the greenhouse was virtually derelict, most of its Gothic detailing removed and much of the glazing gone. The Trust has undertaken a program to halt further deterioration of this gothicized Victorian landmark, and hopes eventually to restore it to fruitful use.

City of Detroit III, a Great Lakes steamer, 1912. Her lounge is now reassembled in the Dossin Great Lakes Museum, Belle Isle, Michigan, as shown here.

Below, Clifford's Burlesque Vaudeville Theatre, White City amusement park, Savin Rock, New Haven.

GOTHIC GRANDEUR

Ralph Adams Cram

For most of his long and incredibly productive career, Ralph Adams Cram (1863–1942) was the chief American exponent of the Gothic style, and few architects have created a legacy of comparable quality. He was the leader of that early twentieth-century school of designers who worked in the purest Medieval idiom to be seen in this country. The son of a New Hampshire Unitarian clergyman, he received his training with the Boston firm of Arthur Rotch and George Tilden, and having completed his apprenticeship, traveled extensively in Europe. In 1888 he formed his own Boston firm with Charles Francis Wentworth.

Cram had always taken a great interest in Gothic architecture. He had read all of Ruskin (Venice was to him "pure beauty"), but like Pugin's, his architectural principles were associated with religious conviction, and he believed that the Gothic style, symbolic of northern and western Christianity for half a millennium, could remain viable if practitioners would "pick up the threads of a broken tradition." A strain of Yankee shrewdness was also evident in his approach, for at the outset of his career he had decided that in order to make his mark he would have to find "some comparatively virgin field" on which to base his practice. He saw that the American resurgence of Gothic stimulated by Ruskin and Pugin had been abruptly halted by the Romanesque Revival, and perceiving a dearth of experts in ecclesiastical Gothic, and encouraged by his own inclinations, he fixed on Gothic churches as the specialty of his firm. It was a happy decision, and probably the most important factor in its success was his conviction that he embodied a continuing architectural tradition of the Middle Ages. He believed that the Gothic had been untimely interrupted "by the synchronizing of the Classical Renaissance and the Protestant Revolution," and felt "that the thing for me to do was to take up the English Gothic at the point where it was cut off during the reign of Henry VIII and go from that point, developing the style

England had made her own, . . . with due regards to the changing conditions of contemporary custom. This of course meant using the English Perpendicular Gothic . . . as the basis of what we hoped to do."

He early received a series of commissions, chiefly for Episcopal churches, of which the first was All Saints, Ashmont, Massachusetts, in 1891. In 1893 the thriving firm took in its talented draftsman Bertram Grosvenor Goodhue (1864–1924) as a partner, and Goodhue's genius for Gothic detailing offset Cram's tendency merely to "reproduce" rather than to "recreate" with new expressions of the form. Wentworth died in 1899, and his place was filled by Frank Ferguson (1861–1926), who acted as the firm's business manager and engineer; thus the triumvirate of Cram, Goodhue, and Ferguson was formed. It gained a national reputation in 1902, with the Gothic entry that won the competition for the expansion of the United States Military Academy at West Point. The crowning touch of the scheme was the Cadet Chapel, a huge, robust Gothic edifice designed by Goodhue for a dramatic site on the cliffs above the Hudson, selected by Cram. The West Point venture brought other commissions, among them St. Thomas' Church in New York, Calvary Episcopal Church in Pittsburgh, and the Euclid Avenue Presbyterian Church in Cleveland.

Goodhue amicably withdrew from the association in 1913 to open his own office in New York, and the firm thereafter continued as Cram and Ferguson. Goodhue's defection did not weaken its prestige, for Cram was by that time known as the leading Gothicist in the United States. His buildings are characterized by sophisticated design, quality of materials, and exquisite craftsmanship; above all, each one has an intangible rightness, evidence of Cram's almost uncanny ability to find the most visually satisfying solution to every problem. Churches and schools remained his specialty, and to have a Cram building became a source of pride to an institution or community. Cram was Supervising Architect for Princeton University from 1909 until 1930, and held similar posts at Bryn Mawr, Mount Holyoke, and the University of Richmond. In the Oxonian idiom, introduced by Cope and Stewardson in the 1890s, he made English Collegiate Gothic the image for schools throughout the country, but the culmination of his career came when he was asked to complete the Cathedral of St. John the Divine.

Cram believed that he was carrying on the evolution of English Medieval architecture from the point where it was halted by the Reformation, but the inspiration for most of his Gothic designs stems from the fourteenth and fifteenth centuries, if not earlier. For all its consistency, his work was not truly consistent with his credo, for most of it lacks the inventiveness of a Burges or a Gilbert Scott. This is true of most of Cram's contemporary American Gothicists: Cope and Stewardson, Day and Klauder, Philip Frohman, and James Gamble Rogers (q.v.) all shunned experiment in favor of the tried and true. But if their Gothic is academic, it is no less beautiful for that. Cram and his fellows may not have

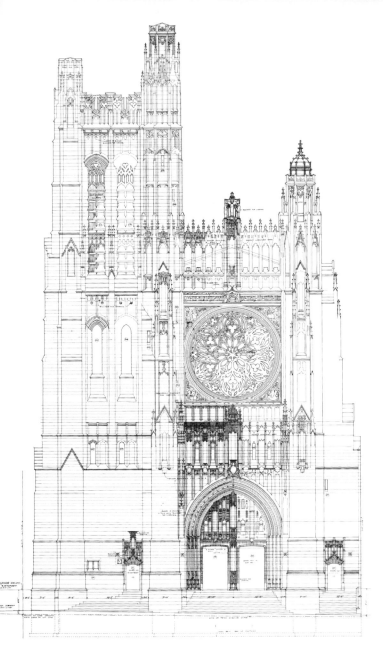

created much that was new, but what they did, they did well, and they have enriched our landscapes with strikingly handsome buildings. Their churches, schools, and residences, gracefully proportioned and solidly constructed, retain an enduring dignity even as many of the more experimental essays of this century begin to look depressingly dated.

Among the most conspicuous and acclaimed works of Cram's firm is the exquisite St. Thomas' Church on Fifth Avenue, built to replace Richard Upjohn's church which was destroyed by fire. With its richly Flamboyant exterior and intricate rose window, the church marks a rare instance in which the partners departed from the usual English precedent and followed French models. The interior, however, is purposefully plain so as not to compete with the huge reredos, which has been called one of the greatest accomplishments of modern ecclesiastical art, far surpassing its Medieval counterparts in scale and magnificence. Although the church itself is largely Cram's (Goodhue made no secret of his distaste for Cram's tendency toward French Gothic), the reredos is entirely of

St. Thomas' Church, New York, 1911–13. Left, east elevation, from Cram, Goodhue, and Ferguson Right, reredos.

149

Graduate College,
Princeton University, New Jersey,
completed in 1913, the refectory

Goodhue's design, and follows the English Perpendicular model. The ivory-colored figures were carved of Dunville stone by Lee Lawrie. This screen, perhaps more than any other single work of Cram's school, exemplifies the timeless beauty that may emerge from the synthesis of scholarship, craftsmanship, imagination, and faith.

Cram's best-known collegiate work is the great University Chapel at Princeton (1925–28), but his ingenuity as a designer is probably better demonstrated in the Graduate College of that university. According to his own account, this commission provided the most spacious opportunity ever enjoyed by his office to work out the concepts and principles of Collegiate Gothic as adapted to modern conditions. The whole complex is beautifully contrived and crafted, and although it seems somewhat anachronistic today, it still perfectly fulfills its function of providing a dignified and commodious home for a fraternity of scholars. Cram's reverence for academe is splendidly illustrated in the main interior space, the refectory. A considerably expanded version of the dining halls of Oxford and Cambridge, the chamber is crowned by the finest hammer-beam ceiling in the country. Cram modestly noted that its trusses were constructed of "solid and honest balks of timber without recourse to hidden steel in any place."

The stylistic and constructional history of the Cathedral Church of St. John the Divine, in which Cram played a major role, is of an irregularity comparable to its Medieval predecessors. Bishop Horatio Potter first dreamed of it in 1873, at a time when great cathedrals, in the European sense, were practically unknown to

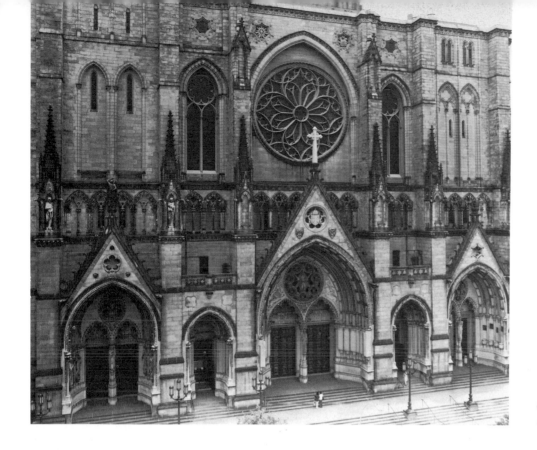

Cathedral Church of St. John the Divine, New York, begun in 1892

American Episcopalianism. The site on Morningside Heights in New York was acquired in 1887, and a competition was held for the design. The winning scheme, combining the fashionable Romanesque and Norman styles, was submitted by the firm of Heins and LaFarge. In 1892 the cornerstone was laid, and work continued until 1907, when Heins died and LaFarge assumed full responsibility. With the completion of the choir in 1911, however, the trustees called a halt. Cram has described how this came about, and why:

> During the elapsed quarter century, the Gothic impulse has been working steadily in the ecclesiastical consciousness. The Romanesque fashion had entirely gone out, after its brief dominion, and the Cathedral authorities had convinced themselves that it was some sort of Gothic that must be used for the continuation of the work. The death of the senior member of the original firm gave them an opportunity to invoke a clause in the contract between the Cathedral and its architect, which provided that, in such event, the contract might at their discretion, be terminated. The action was taken and I was asked to go on from that point.

So it was that our foremost Gothic architect accepted, on behalf of his firm, the commission to complete what in cubic feet was to be the second largest church in the world. (Ironically, Cram had entered the original competition with a rather chunky Romanesque scheme.) The firm's Gothic design for the completion was of mature, self-confident grandeur, albeit highly conservative. It was basically composed of more or less standard French and English elements, skillfully worked into the existing Romanesque apse. Certain innovations were introduced; the side aisles, for example, were raised to the height of the nave, so that the clerestory windows are separated by the full width of the church, instead of only by the width of the nave, as in most Medieval churches. When the Second World War

151

Cathedral Church of Bryn Athyn,
Montgomery County,
Pennsylvania, 1913–19

halted construction, the nave (surely one of the most awesome spaces in the western hemisphere) and the west front, minus the towers, had been completed. The crossing had only a temporary covering and the transepts did not exist. Since that time various plans for completion have been proposed, but the sharpened social conscience of recent years has obliged the Church to give priority to other financial commitments. Suggestions for simplifying the design have included capping the unfinished portions with large unornamented buttresses, as an appropriate modern compromise. In 1973, at the centennial of the Cathedral's founding, it was announced that construction would resume, but that a scheme had not been agreed upon.

When commissioned to design the episcopal seat of the Swedenborgian Church, Cram instituted the two innovations that raise the Cathedral above all other Gothic Revival churches as an expression of Medieval art and aspirations. The first was the establishment of a quasi-guild system that involved bringing together all the building's designers and craftsmen, and grouping them in workshops and studios around the actual building, according to the custom of the Middle Ages. Cram wanted the work done in the Medieval manner, by one body of craftsmen devoting their full attention to a project evolving day by day out of a communal effort. Under these conditions the artisans could understand, analyze, and criticize one another's work and thereby make the Cathedral the best possible expression of a unified endeavor.

Cram also decided to introduce into the building the optical refinements shown by scholarly examination to have been used in the more sophisticated Medieval churches. He therefore designed the Cathedral so that pavement of the nave slopes slightly upward toward the chancel, and so that the intercolumniations vary in

152

every bay. He also made the nave's piers, arcades, and walls not rectilinear in alignment, but with subtle curves concave to the nave, and employed entasis in the piers framing the sanctuary, as well as in the main tower. The facade of the entrance porch was given a convex bend in plan as well as a slight backward slanting curve in its elevation. All of this was done not out of affectation, but "because we felt sure that of old it was done with a purpose, and we wanted to find out what that was, and if it would work." This was the first modern church building to make use of such refinements, but it is probably also the last; Cram lamented that this type of design was too expensive for both architect and client.

Cram was enabled to institute his novel system of building at Bryn Athyn by John Pitcairn, who donated the considerable cost of construction and who was in complete sympathy with Cram's ideas. Pitcairn died shortly after work commenced, and his son Raymond began to exercise a strong influence on the work. His involvement soon put him at odds with Cram, who naturally wanted the last say in particulars and felt that Pitcairn was causing him to lose control of decision making. Pitcairn wanted to keep the plans and designs in a state of flux so as to assure evolution of the building through the continued collaboration of all the designers and workmen. He finally prevailed, and Cram was released from the project after three years of construction. The main body of the Cathedral was completed in 1919 under Pitcairn's direction, and work on many of its details, executed in the cooperative spirit initiated by Cram, continues.

Despite his dismissal Cram remained enthusiastic about the project, and it is he who best, though immodestly, expresses its place in the American Gothic Revival: "the result is not only unique but one of the most picturesque and romantic architectural compositions in the country. It is a sort of epitome of English church-building from the earliest Norman to the latest Perpendicular; learned, scholarly, poetic; a real masterpiece of reminiscent yet creative art."

The St. George's School Chapel, in Middletown, Rhode Island, ranks among the most magnificent preparatory school chapels in the United States; its tower is one of the few structures for which Cram actually did the drawing. It was the gift of an alumnus, John Nicholas Brown of the class of 1918, who made this generous gesture as his first public act upon coming of age, and it was completed in 1928. Brown took an active interest in the scheme, and assisted the firm in working out the symbolism, criticizing the plans, and even designing portions of the pavement. Since St. George's is an Episcopal school, Cram felt the chapel's design to be a problem "facile of solution," feeling that "Gothic followed, as a matter of course, and of the type that William of Wyckham, that great statesman, educator, and amateur architect, was largely instrumental in bringing into existence." Playing the Medievalist, Cram had the bosses carved with personifications of schoolboy slang—"lounge-lizards," "bookworms," and the like. Also among the carvings are representations of ships of the East India trade, the ancestral source of the donor's wealth.

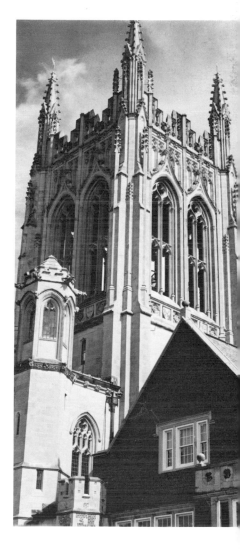

St. George's School Chapel, Middletown, Rhode Island, 1924–28

153

FOR GOD, FOR RINGLING, & FOR YALE

Harkness Tower, Yale University, New Haven, 1917–21

CRAM AND HIS followers breathed new life into the Gothic Revival, giving it a stature it had not enjoyed since the Middle Ages. Although the eclectic architectural spirit of the time created a welcoming climate, public reawakening toward the style was largely owed to a single, modest book, *Mont St. Michel and Chartres*, by Henry Adams. Privately printed in 1903, and later published commercially at Cram's insistence, it became a perennial bestseller and nurtured a genuine reverence for the Gothic that is still very much with us today. Adams's attribution of divine inspiration to the style had a powerful impact; thereafter, although Gothic was still employed on what might be thought of as frivolous works, few architects dared to flout integrity of structure and materials in Gothic essays. An Edwardian edifice commissioned for no more worthy purpose than to outshine its neighbors still conveyed the serious scholarship of its designer.

This apotheosis of Gothic served to stimulate its use. In fact, it is not absurd to speculate that more of our buildings in the style may date from after the turn of this century than from all the years before. The stream of churches, schools, office buildings, and residences ranged from such a vast complex as the University of Chicago, by Henry Ives Cobb, to a simple Gothic frontispiece on a plain brick apartment house. Cram's beloved English Gothic, particularly the Perpendicular and Tudor modes, once again became the primary source; continental forms remained largely absent from the vocabulary, except (thanks to Adams) for occasional French influences.

In 1900 Cope and Stewardson, noted for their Tudor exercises at Princeton and Bryn Mawr, won a competition for the first buildings at Washington University, and sent their draftsman James F. Jamieson to St. Louis to establish a branch office and supervise construction. The plan called for a complex that would have been at home on the banks of the Cam or the Cherwell. When Walter Cope died in 1902, Jamieson became the official Washington University architect. One of his most striking contributions to the campus is Graham Chapel, adapted from the chapel at Eton College. The ogival turrets are inspired by those at King's College, Cambridge, but the ceiling is timbered, as at Eton, rather than fan-vaulted as at King's. Jamieson (1867–1941) has a number of other buildings in the Tudor style to his credit; Memorial Tower at the University of Missouri, built in 1927, is one of the best known.

A number of schools put up Gothic buildings as late as the 1950s, and a few are doing so today, although chiefly to complete master plans laid out years ago. Probably the most notable collegiate complex, in both design and execution, is the Memorial Quadrangle at Yale, of which James Gamble Rogers (1867–1947) was the architect; it boasts stonework of an aesthetic quality unmatched in any similar American concourse. Harkness Tower, highlight of the complex, is another one of the rare instances of French precedent in collegiate design; Talbot Hamlin hailed its sweeping verticality as "a brilliant departure from the square Oxford variety." Images of every famous scholar, allegorical figure, and eminent alumnus for whom space could be found were worked into its ornamentation.

The examples set by Yale, Princeton, and Chicago had far-reaching effects. An historical atmosphere became inextricably associated with education, and accordingly, Gothic came to be applied in nearly every sort of school building, including gymnasiums and power plants. Nearly every city built at least one public school with some degree of Gothic decoration, and almost every twentieth-century military school has a castellated air. Few of these buildings are masterpieces, but as a whole they form an architectural phenomenon yet to receive adequate study.

Graham Chapel,
Washington University,
St. Louis, Missouri, 1909.
Right, detail of organ case.

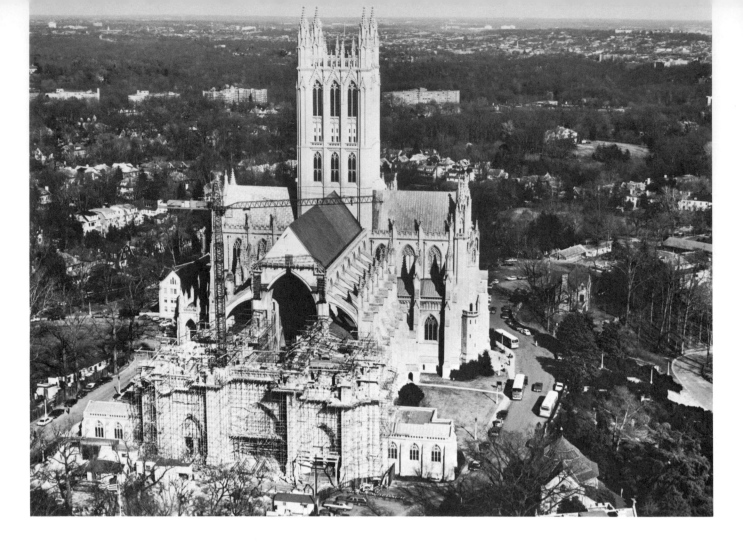

Washington Cathedral, begun in 1907

Our continuing ecclesiastical Gothic tradition is nowhere better shown than in the Cathedral Church of St. Peter and St. Paul in Washington, D.C., better known as Washington Cathedral. This masterpiece of the Gothic revival has been under construction since 1907; masons, stone-carvers, and other artisans still employ their specialized skills, striving to complete the building by 1980. The project may be the colossal anachronism it has been called, but it is undeniably a glorious celebration of traditional Christian art and architecture.

George Washington envisioned a great church for the Capitol, and Pierre L'Enfant allowed space for it near the Mall, but the actual site for the Cathedral was not chosen until 1893, when the Protestant Episcopal Cathedral Foundation was formed by Act of Congress, and in its turn established the Diocese of Washington. The first Bishop, Henry Yates Satterlee, chose Mount Alban, overlooking the city to the south, so that the Cathedral would be a landmark floating serenely over the bustle of Washington.

A Renaissance scheme was briefly considered for the design, but was overruled in favor of the English Gothic, thought more appropriate for an Episcopal building. The roster of architects associated with the Cathedral is impressive. Bishop Satterlee felt that an experienced British Gothicist was called for, and accepted the Archbishop of Canterbury's recommendation of George Frederick Bodley (q.v.). There was strong partisanship among the clergy, however, for Henry Vaughan (q.v.), and in the end both men were retained as associates. Their collaboration produced a plan in the English Decorated style, a relatively standard scheme with a cruciform ground plan, twin west towers, and a large

156

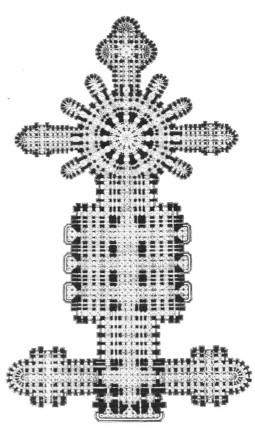

crossing tower ornamented with corner pinnacles. Then Bodley died, shortly after preliminary drawings were made, and Vaughan survived the placing of the foundation stone in 1907 by only ten years. Bishop and Dean thereupon determined to seek competent younger men to continue the project, and appointed a trio including Philip Hubert Frohman, Donald Robb, and Harry Little; Cram's firm was to serve as consultant. Both Robb and Little had trained under Cram. The new team decided that the Cathedral design did not represent the highest standard of Bodley's or Vaughan's oeuvre, perhaps because neither architect had previously worked upon so large a scale. At that time only Vaughan's lovely Bethlehem Chapel and portions of the apse walls above it had been completed. Without altering the basic overall concept, the young associates made adjustments in proportion and detail in order to achieve what Cram called "the most perfect example of pure English fourteenth-century architecture that has come into being since that century closed." By the middle '40s, both Robb and Little had died, and Frohman became the Cathedral Architect, a title he held until his retirement in 1971; his name is inseparable from the still-growing edifice. Frohman's former associate, Howard Trevillian, is now directing the completion.

The Washington Cathedral is truly a monumental undertaking. It will be the fifth largest cathedral in the world, and every detail from masonry to stained glass hews as closely as possible to Medieval example and precept. Despite some pressures, no departure has yet been made from the original concept or its manner of execution. Here, Gothic architecture may be observed at its purest and most grand. It testifies to Frohman's expressed hope that it "may be a stepping-stone to

Delaware & Hudson Railroad Company Building, Albany, 1914–18

a development of Gothic architecture in the future . . . which will be greater and more beautiful than any single period of the past."

The concept of the Washington Cathedral may have satisfied the general public desire for a fitting national church, but to one man at least it was not enough. Charles Mason Remey therefore designed in 1929 a nondenominational "National Church and Shrine," to be situated, as a continuation of the axis of the Capitol and Mall, on the west bank of the Potomac. Remey's designs for a Gothic church over a quarter of a mile in length exceed the incredible; predictably, his drawings have never gotten beyond the basement of the Avery Architectural Library at Columbia.

Remey's visionary project remains unrealized, but a great number of effectively designed and well-executed Gothic buildings of this century do exist. A commercial example is the Delaware & Hudson Railroad Company Building in Albany. Most American railroad station–office building combinations in the Gothic style date from the nineteenth century; the Delaware & Hudson Building is something of a survival, having been put up during the First World War. It was designed by the local architect Marcus T. Reynolds, who contrived a large reinforced-concrete and steel-framed structure, with a Franco-Teutonic skin and a tall square central tower with corner turrets. This tower is balanced at the southerly end of the building by a polygonal tower which is part of the wing erected for the *Albany Evening Journal*. The edifice is an important element in an ambitious 1910 plan to improve downtown Albany, and was intended to climax the view down State Street. The megalithic structures of the city's redevelopment scheme make the older building, in spite of its monumental scale and strategic location, appear almost quaint. It is being remodeled to house a college.

Gothic regained its popularity for domestic building in the early twentieth century, although in somewhat different forms from those of the nineteenth. For the successful, the mode christened by Osbert Lancaster "Stockbrokers Tudor" became a symbol of affluence, expressed in sprawling Elizabethan manor houses, while humbler aspirations were met in careful reproductions of diminutive Cotswold cottages. Most of these houses were designed with extreme care, in order to insure the all-important historical flavor. This antiquarianism was occasionally carried to extremes. Welsh slate was imported, machine-cut timbers adzed to look hand-hewn, and calculated sags introduced in perfectly sound roofs; in several instances complete English houses were imported and reerected in exclusive suburbs. For those in really modest circumstances there were simple two-story homes or row houses bravely decked out in half-timbering, casement windows, and Gothic moldings. Venetian and Spanish Gothic, suited to the climate, flourished in Florida and California; at Florida resorts Venetian was considered especially stylish; in quality these latter-day palazzi range from comfortable elegance to pure theatrics.

Many contemporary architects declined to identify themselves with any one period or style. John Russell Pope was a leader of this eclectic school. With equal deftness he produced the smoothly Classical Jefferson Memorial in Washington, D.C., and richly textured Tudor houses on both cottage and baronial scales. A characteristic example of his Tudor work is the Richmond mansion designed for John Kerr Branch as the setting for a collection of art and antiques. So flawless was Pope's scholarship that a visitor from sixteenth-century England would feel perfectly at home with the house, at least until he spied the large monument to Jefferson Davis that dominates the intersection in front.

Acceptance of eclecticism produced some extraordinary ventures in house design, in which Gothic forms played their part. Playa Riente, one of the largest houses ever built in Palm Beach, was one of the few on the ocean; the ballroom balcony overhung the beach. It was put up in 1923 for Joshua Cosden by Addison Mizner, at a cost of $1,800,000. As an architect, Mizner was much attracted by the Spanish modes he had found in Guatemala, but was reluctant to be tied to any one style even in the same building, so that he would "sometimes start a house with a Romanesque corner, pretend that it has fallen into disrepair and been added to in the Gothic spirit, when suddenly the great wealth of the New World has poured in and the owner [has] added a very rich Renaissance addition." He designed the home for convalescent servicemen that became the Everglades Club, and was then commissioned to do the elaborate Stotesbury estate; thereafter everyone craved a Mizner creation. He produced in his own workshops a variety of suitably antiqued materials for his buildings—roofing tiles, floor tiles, ironwork, furniture—to harmonize with ancient fragments from Europe. At Playa Riente the entrance hall, reminiscent of Beckford's hall at Fonthill Abbey, filled the central block, with a grand stairway leading to the main floor. From it, opposite the front door, a tunnel ran under the terrace to the beach. The dining room was frescoed by Achille Angeli, the ballroom later decorated by José Sert. The house was demolished by its second owner, Mrs. Horace Dodge, Sr., in 1957, when staffing such establishments had become an almost insuperable problem. Fragments of the building survive in the Pamela Prehler Memorial Studio and the Graham–Eckes School in Palm Beach, and in the Driftwood Inn in Vero Beach.

Branch House, Richmond, 1916

Top right, Playa Riente, Palm Beach, Florida, 1923. (The Florida Architecture of Addison Mizner, 1928)

Top left, Mar-a-Lago, Palm Beach, 1923–27

Right, Ca' d'Zan, Sarasota, Florida, 1926

Designed by Marion Sims Wyeth for Mrs. Marjorie Merriweather Post, Mar-a-Lago survives as the most lavish of the grand Palm Beach resort houses. The sprawling exterior reflects the Hispano-Moorish style popularized in Florida by Carrère and Hastings in their Ponce de Leon Hotel in St. Augustine. The interior designer was Joseph Urban, a Viennese with a distinguished career on two continents as illustrator, architect, and set designer. His *pièce de resistance* at Mar-a-Lago is the opulent Venetian Gothic "Gold Room." The 42-foot ceiling, covered in gold leaf, is copied from the "Thousand-Wing" ceiling in the Accademia in Venice. The rest of the decoration is freely adapted from Venetian and Spanish Gothic motifs. The room focuses on a great arched window made from a single sheet of plate glass, one of the largest ever fabricated. Mrs. Post willed Mar-a-Lago to the federal government, and it is now in the charge of the National Park Service.

Mizner, the great architectural showman, reigned supreme in the field of resort house design on the east coast of Florida. But when that incomparable showman John Ringling chose an architect to create his showplace facing Sarasota Bay, he commissioned Dwight James Baum, of New York, another eclectic architect with a wide domestic practice. Baum was versed in many styles; at Ca' d'Zan he produced a Venetian palazzo, combining terra cotta, marbles, and antique red roof tiles with stucco to achieve the effect the Ringlings sought. Mrs. Ringling wanted a Spanish tower like the one on the old Madison Square Garden, but was obliged to compromise on a modest version of it; however, the Gothic observatory that tops the tower still dominates the local skyline. The interior court is rimmed by a gallery, the entrance side supported on Gothic arches. Ceiled in with pecky cypress and lit by a great skylight, it served as the living room. Much of the Gavet collection from the Gothic Room at Marble House (q.v.) is now at Ca' d'Zan. The house and adjoining museum are open to the public.

Florida also boasts a particularly elegant and uncluttered example of the Gothic style dating from the 1920s. When he created the Mountain Lake bird sanctuary, Edward Bok called on a fellow Philadelphian, Milton B. Medary, to design a carillon tower as its focal point. The result is an exotic but poetically beautiful campanile of pink and gray Georgia marble with ribs of native coquina. Although Medary is better known for such familiar landmarks as the Cosmos Club in Washington, D.C., and the Valley Forge Chapel, his Singing Tower won the American Institute of Architects' Gold Medal in 1929. The tower is Gothic in form and outline, and its details are highly original works of sculpture. The naturalistic tracery in the arches takes the form of native trees, and the pinnacles are stylized birds of local species. The sanctuary itself was planned by Frederick Law Olmsted.

This late and variegated flowering of the Gothic Revival culminated in Duke Chapel (1930–35), the last and grandest essay in twentieth-century ecclesiastical campus Gothic. James Buchanan Duke, founder of the American Tobacco Company, was of the opinion that religion lies at the heart of education, and when he transformed a small North Carolina college into the splendid, if sprawling, Gothic complex appropriately renamed Duke University, he intended a vast chapel to dominate the symmetrical plan of the campus; it is linked by symbolic arcades to the academic buildings on either side. The entire complex was designed by Horace Trumbauer (1869–1938), a leader of the eclectic school, whose works range in mode from the neo-Georgian Widener Library at Harvard to the Louis XV-style Free Library in Philadelphia. Oddly enough, until he received the Duke commission, Trumbauer had not been especially noted as a Gothicist. The chapel is architecturally correct to the last finial, but is unconventional in the distribution of its major parts. The main tower, instead of rising over the crossing, behind a facade with two towers or none, itself composes the entire facade. It is modeled on the Bell Harry Tower at Canterbury Cathedral, and is as wide as the side aisles and buttresses of the nave, so that viewed axially it might almost be taken for a separate structure. The interior, 291 feet in length and carrying the characteristic ridge rib down the center of its English-style rib-and-panel vaulting, forms an impressive vista.

Singing Tower,
Mountain Lake Sanctuary,
Lake Wales, Florida, 1929

Duke Chapel, Duke University,
Durham, North Carolina, 1930–35,
exterior and nave

SHINING
TOWERS

Jayne Building, Philadelphia, 1851.
(Pennsylvania Historical Society)

THE PROTOTYPE OF the American skyscraper, completed in 1851, was unfortunately torn down in 1957. Designed by William L. Johnston as a shop and warehouse for Dr. Davis Jayne, a purveyor of patent medicines, the building was ten stories in height, a dimension that the architect emphasized by applying granite clustered piers to the facade. These extended from the first floor to the top stories, terminating in pointed arches and quatrefoils in a Venetian manner. The roof walk was crowned with a two-story castellated tower, still further accenting the rectilinear verticality of the structure.

Johnston here demonstrated the eminent suitability of the Gothic style for multistory buildings, but it was not much employed for them until the early years of the twentieth century. In the 1870s through the '90s, formative years in skyscraper design, most great office blocks were built to a French or Italian Renaissance formula, generally displaying either great mansard roofs or flat roofs with deep cornices. The majority followed in composition a tripartite system based on the proportional relationship of the pedestal, shaft, and capital of a Classical column. Richardson's Romanesque Revival buildings had a significant influence on skyscraper design, and in Chicago, Louis Sullivan and his fellows evolved the "Commercial" style for such buildings, avoiding practically all historical associations.

Except in isolated cases, most architects eschewed the Gothic for skyscrapers until Cass Gilbert completed the Woolworth Building in 1913. A few large Gothic Masonic temples had been erected in major cities, and the Ruskinian Gothic influence had lingered on in the design of a handful of commercial structures, but few of these were in the skyscraper class. The prestige and magnitude of the Woolworth Building encouraged other architects to give a Gothic aspect to their huge commercial centers, but while Gilbert's masterpiece of proportion and decoration inspired a number of Gothic towers, the Classical and afterward the Modernist modes continued to dominate skyscraper design. With the exceptions of Chicago's Tribune Tower, the General Electric Building in New York, and one or two others, most skyscrapers of Gothic inspiration erected after the First World War appear vapid beside their few earlier counterparts. It took singular vision and ability to transfer the vitality of a basically ecclesiastical style to these super-tall temples of Mammon; those who lacked the requisite talent produced little more than bland shafts sprinkled with a few superficial pointed details. Some architects were, however, inspired by the upward thrust of Gothic forms and the vitality of their details to abstract these motifs into the almost pure geometric style now known as Art Deco.

The Chicago firm of Holabird and Roche pioneered the use of steel-skeleton framing, and its buildings are more noted for how they are constructed than for how they look. But while most of the firm's works, particularly the Tacoma Building, show little historicism, the University Club (1910) is clothed in full-blown Collegiate Tudor—an example of the powerful affinity of that Gothic mode for any academically oriented structure, and one of the first occasions where the Gothic style was adapted for the adornment of a tall major building. Often ridiculed by architectural critics, who like to think of Chicago's buildings as memorable for forward-looking originality rather than eclecticism, the University Club succeeds by firmly declaring itself for what it is; and lest some passerby foolishly associate it with commerce, the architects placed owls of wisdom at the peaks of its gables. Holabird and Roche employed their Gothic ornaments in a very literal manner, quite unlike the considerable abstraction necessitated in later, much larger, buildings by the need to sustain a credible composition.

Frank Woolworth conceived the idea of raising the world's tallest building for his corporate headquarters largely as a huge advertisement for his five-and-ten-cent stores. For his architect he selected Cass Gilbert (1858–1934), who had recently won renown for the New York Customs House and had already demonstrated his ability to handle Manhattan skyscraper design with the Broadway–Chambers Building and the West Street Building. In planning for a structure of such unprecedented height, Gilbert departed from his customary tripartite scheme and proposed an isolated tower soaring thirty stories above the front of a twenty-five story block. His use of a Gothic decorative theme in the embellishment of the building was successful; Louis Horowitz, contractor for the Woolworth Building, described Gilbert as "the first architect ever to contrive a scale to give the Gothic quality of lace in stone to a building of supernormal proportions." Gilbert skillfully adjusted his ornament to the towering vertical lines so that the perspective succeeds as well close up as from a distance. Much of this visual success derives from the white terra cotta which was the architect's inspired

choice of sheathing material. As critic Montgomery Schuyler pointed out, cut stone would have had to be handled in a fashion contrary to its nature in order to conform to the design of so large a building, whereas terra cotta had the flexibility necessary for application to this enormous pile.

The Woolworth Building became not only a symbol of a great corporation, but a monument to the ego of a self-made multimillionaire. Woolworth was not content merely to impress the populace with the power of his wealth; he wanted to overwhelm it. While the project was in the planning stage he let it be known that the building would measure 692 feet, at that time a world's record. That it actually was to be a hundred feet higher was a secret kept until the last moment, just so he could elicit an extra gasp of awe. He naturally provided himself with a marble office of appropriate majesty, furnished in the French Empire taste, with a full-length portrait of Napoleon hung where the magnate's eye would fall upon it. In all justice, Woolworth had a right to be proud of his "Cathedral of Commerce." Even now, when office blocks several hundred feet higher are common, it remains our greatest aesthetic achievement in skyscraper design.

Many architectural historians discuss the competition for the design of the Chicago Tribune Tower in terms of an opportunity lost, a step backward in the history of American design. But although such architects as Walter Gropius and Eliel Saarinen entered the competition only to lose, and the winning design by Howells and Hood is certainly no forerunner of the bleak monoliths that overpower our city skylines today, the building has its own value. Dispassionately viewed, it is a major achievement in skyscraper design, one best appreciated in the context of its times. It was built in celebration of the seventy-fifth anniversary of

Left to right:
University Club,
Chicago, 1910;
Woolworth Building,
New York, 1911–13;
Chicago Tribune Building,
1922–25.

*Cathedral of Learning,
University of Pittsburgh,
1926–27*

the founding of the *Chicago Tribune*, and the competition for the design was intended to secure for the newspaper and Chicago both a monument to progress and "the most beautiful building in the world," a model for future generations of newspaper publishers and ordinary citizens. The *Tribune* was very serious about the project. Prizes totaling $100,000 were offered, and although some of the leading architects in the country were invited to enter, the competition was open to all. The challenge was so exciting that no fewer than 189 architects, many from European firms, submitted designs. All entries were anonymous, and the judges went to great lengths to assure their own absolute impartiality.

The entries form a remarkable cross-section of current fashions in skyscrapers during the 1920s. Twenty-nine schemes have a distinctly Gothic character or rely heavily on Gothic motifs, and several of these received honorable mention, among them the proposals of Rogers, Goodhue, and Guy Lowell. A large proportion of the entries fell into the rich Beaux-Arts tradition or a more restrained Classicism; a few were Egyptian. Others, particularly several from Europe, were wholly modernistic. In all, the designs ranged from the sublime to the ridiculous; one proposal called for a skyscraper in the shape of an American Indian chief. The building was erected to the winning scheme of John Mead Howells and Raymond Hood of New York. Second prize went to Eliel Saarinen of Finland for a strikingly handsome design that was not devoid of certain Gothic overtones and won the unqualified praise of Louis Sullivan. The third prize was given to a Gothic scheme submitted by Holabird and Roche. It is easy to understand why the Howells and Hood concept was the most acceptable in 1922 to a jury of architects and businessmen seeking to create the "most beautiful building in the world." Obvious and timeless aesthetics, no jarring note of modernity or florid ostentation, was what was wanted. At that time Gothic appeared to be an almost infallible formula, the most sublime expression of architecture. By the judicious combination of Gothic motifs and impeccable proportions, Howells and Hood achieved a work of conservative grandeur profoundly appealing to its sponsors.

The Babel of twentieth-century Collegiate Gothic is Charles Z. Klauder's skyscraper for the University of Pittsburgh. Combining idealism, historicism, and technology, the great edifice was conceived as a true cathedral of learning—a focal point of inspiration where the many nationalities of the city could acquire education and culture. Symbolic values outweighed functional considerations in the design, with the result that it is notorious for congested elevators and impassable halls during class changes. Thomas Jefferson had shown, as far back as the 1820s, that the "academical village" has many advantages over a single building for a university plan. Nevertheless, Klauder (1872–1938) was an able Gothicist, and from a strictly visual standpoint his building is notably graceful. His skillfully handled Gothic details credibly embellish a twentieth-century form.

GOTHIC FOR TODAY

Dutch Wonderland, Lancaster, Pennsylvania, 1963

THE ECHO OF the Gothic mood still gently reverberates. The style is yet called upon, from time to time, to impart the feeling of a make-believe world believably peopled with knights and dragons, giants and dwarfs. In such refuges from reality as the Disney utopias of Florida and California, or the Dutch Wonderland in Pennsylvania, Gothic forms are used to set the stage for the most up-to-the-minute amusements, comfortably laced with nostalgia. In some serious contemporary works, however, a certain lightness and grace has been achieved by the delicate use of Gothic forms. Few modern architects have consciously attempted to give their works specific historical overtones, but slender structural elements, strong verticality, and pointed motifs nevertheless impart a strong Gothic feeling. The architects of such buildings might well deny any derivative inspiration; one may still conclude that had there never been a Gothic style, these structures would convey quite a different impression, not least in the eye of the beholder.

Sometimes the reminiscent quality is serendipitous. Laminated wood arches, often seen in modern churches, mark the appearance of a new structural system, which at the same time recalls the totally different systems of the Middle Ages. In Zion Lutheran Church, Portland, Oregon, Pietro Belluschi employed a framework of laminated wood arches to support the roof. By placing the bases of free-standing arches three feet in from the outer wall, he created side aisles, reducing the width of the interior span. Consequently, the curve of the supporting members becomes shallower and the visual effect is that of a pointed arch.

The Cadet Chapel of the United States Air Force Academy was designed by Walter Netsch of Skidmore, Owings & Merrill. Using contemporary materials and the latest construction methods, the architect has evoked the aspiring quality of a Medieval church. The Protestant Chapel was created by assembling 100 aluminum tetrahedrons into a triangular structure 150 feet high with 17 spires; the strict geometry of the form is a sharp contrast to the rugged scenery surrounding it. The interior is lit by narrow strips of stained glass between the aluminum spires; color is added through the use of terrazzo, marble, and warm woods.

Above left, Zion Lutheran Church, Portland, Oregon, 1952

Above right, Cadet Chapel, U. S. Air Force Academy, El Paso County, Colorado, 1959–63

Right, Northwestern National Life Insurance Company, Minneapolis, 1963–64

Minoru Yamasaki, in his design for the Science Pavilion at the Seattle International Exposition of 1962, the Wayne University Conference Building, and his rejected scheme for the United States Embassy in London, has shown continuing interest in Gothic forms. The Northwestern National Life Insurance Company Building, begun in 1963, exemplifies the acknowledgment of Medieval modes displayed by this talented contemporary architect. The columns of the imposing portico are faced with white quartz aggregate concrete, and their flaring tops come together to form a succession of pointed arches. Further vertical accent is provided by additional columns, together with panels of verde-antique marble between the windows. Like the Cadet Chapel, the composition happily calls to mind the soaring quality of the great Gothic cathedrals—the Medieval forms upon which our first builders drew more than three centuries ago, and which have served to support and adorn so much of our building ever since.

EPILOGUE

Stonemason at the Washington Cathedral

THE AUTHORS HAVE attempted to indicate the wide range of American interpretations of the Gothic style, and to trace the course of our changing attitudes toward it; in closing, it seems appropriate to glance at its current status in this country. Respect for pure Medieval Gothic has certainly not waned; authentic specimens appear to defy criticism. But save for the essentially unique Washington Cathedral project, interest in the style as a design resource is at an ebb among today's architects. High construction costs, the scarcity of craftsmen, and the rejection of historic styles by most contemporary practitioners have combined to prevent the creation of any new Gothic works of consequence. Gothic overtones do appear in some contemporary buildings, but serious modern essays in the idiom are few and far between. It would be unwise to assume, however, that the Gothic is dead; it has displayed a phoenix-like quality of survival, and we may yet see new interpretations flourish. The present lull, meanwhile, has provided a long-overdue opportunity to appraise American achievements in the style.

For thirty or forty years the Gothic portion of our architectural heritage has been taken largely for granted, so that buildings of that persuasion have attracted far less interest and concern than those in less audacious historical modes. Perhaps the styles of Classical derivation—Georgian, Federal, and Greek Revival—have come to be considered more "American" than Medieval modes; at any rate, disinterest in and even distaste for Gothic has resulted in the irreclaimable loss of a significant number of important structures. In recent years such benchmarks as the Jayne Building, Davis's Harral–Wheeler House, and Myers's Grand Rapids City Hall, have vanished along with scores of less well-known villas, cottages, and public buildings. Churches have suffered least from this rash of demolition, but they doubtless owe their preservation less to admiration of the Gothic than to scanty funds and the inherent conservatism of established religious congregations.

Fashionable disdain for Gothic structures, more particularly those of the mid-nineteenth century, was considerably mitigated in the 1960s. In 1966

The New York Yacht Club en route to a permanent haven at the Mystic Seaport Museum, Connecticut

Sunday morning at Yeocomico Church

Lyndhurst, the premier surviving example of its type, passed to the National Trust for Historic Preservation, and this lent a new respectability to Gothic preservation. Impetus for the movement came in the same year with the passage of the National Historic Preservation Act, establishing the National Register of Historic Places. The National Register encourages each state to submit nominations for registry covering all phases of the state's architectural and historical progress, and a great number of Gothic buildings have thereby received belated recognition as landmarks worthy of protection. These designations, which apply to the majority of the extant buildings illustrated here, have been the major factor in saving a broad spectrum of our Gothic exercises. To be sure, not all important examples are yet secure, but their value is ever more widely recognized.

Some significant buildings have become museums, open to all for study and enjoyment, and others, their original functions outmoded, have been put to imaginative new uses. Many successfully continue to serve the purposes for which they were designed: Gothic school buildings still provide an effective background for educational pursuits, Gothic public buildings sustain themselves as civic symbols, Gothic houses of worship retain their inspiring character, and Gothic residences still function as genial or romantic foils to a workaday world. Across these fifty United States a generous legacy of Medieval inspiration, in every conceivable variation of period, type, and mode, continues to enrich our daily lives and our understanding of the dreams and aspirations of the past.

Lyndhurst,
the Fourth of July

Bibliography

The works listed are those the authors found most helpful in compiling this book. They should assist in giving the reader further insight into the scope and complexity of Gothic architecture in the United States. *The Journal of the Society of Architectural Historians* is abbreviated *JSAH*.

**I
SELECTED
FOREIGN WORKS
INFLUENCING AMERICAN
GOTHIC ARCHITECTURE**

HALFPENNY, WILLIAM and JOHN. *Chinese and Gothic Architecture Properly Ornamented.* London: Sayer, 1752.

LANGLEY, BATTY and THOMAS. *Gothic Architecture Improved by Rules and Proportions in Many Grand Designs . . . .* London: Millan, 1742.

LIGHTOLER, THOMAS. *The Gentleman's and Farmer's Architect.* London: Sayer, 1762.

MEINERT, FRIEDRICH. *Die Schöne Landbaukunst.* Leipzig, 1798.

OVER, CHARLES. *Ornamental Architecture in the Gothic, Chinese and Modern Taste.* London, 1758.

PUGIN, AUGUSTUS CHARLES. *Examples of Gothic Architecture.* London: Bohn, 1831–38.

PUGIN, AUGUSTUS WELBY NORTHMORE. *The True Principles of Pointed or Christian Architecture.* London: Weale, 1841.

RUSKIN, JOHN. *The Seven Lamps of Architecture.* New York: Wiley, 1849.

———. *The Stones of Venice.* New York: Wiley, 1860.

**II
MAJOR AMERICAN
ARCHITECTURAL PATTERN-
BOOKS ILLUSTRATING
AND ADVOCATING
THE GOTHIC STYLE**

ALLEN, LEWIS F. *Rural Architecture.* New York: Saxton, 1852.

ARNOT, DAVID HENRY. *Gothic Architecture Applied to Modern Residences.* New York: Appleton, 1849.

CLEAVELAND, HENRY WILLIAM. *Village and Farm Cottages.* New York: Appleton, 1856.

DAVIS, ALEXANDER JACKSON. *Rural Residences.* New York: 1837.

DOWNING, ANDREW JACKSON. *The Architecture of Country Houses.* New York: Appleton, 1850.

———. *Cottage Residences.* New York: Wiley & Putnam, 1842.

———. *Rural Essays.* New York: Putnam, 1853.

———. *A Treatise on the Theory and Practice of Landscape Gardening, Adapted to North America; . . . With Remarks on Rural Architecture.* New York: Putnam, 1841 and later editions.

HILLS, CHESTER. *The Builder's Guide.* Hartford: Case, Tiffany & Burnham, 1847. 2nd rev. ed.

HOPKINS, JOHN HENRY, BISHOP of VERMONT. *Essay on Gothic Architecture: Designed Chiefly for the Use of the Clergy.* Burlington, Vt.: Smith & Harrington, 1836.

RANLETT, WILLIAM H. *The Architect, A Series of Original Designs for Domestic and Ornamental Villas Adapted to the United States.* New York: Graham, 1847–49.

The Rules of Work of the Carpenters' Company of the City and County of Philadelphia, 1786. Ed. by Charles E. Peterson. Princeton: Pyne Press, 1971. Reprint. Originally titled *Articles of the Carpenters Company of Philadelphia: and Their Rules for Measuring and Valuing House-Carpenters Work* (Philadelphia: Hall and Sellers, 1786).

SLOAN, SAMUEL. *The Model Architect.* Philadelphia: E. G. Jones, 1852.
UPJOHN, RICHARD. *Upjohn's Rural Architecture.* New York: Putnam, 1852.
VAUX, CALVERT. *Villas and Cottages.* New York: Harper, 1864. 2nd ed.
WHEELER, GERVASE. *Rural Homes.* New York: Scribner, 1851.
WOODWARD, GEORGE EVERTSON. *Woodward's Country Homes.* New York: George E. & F. W. Woodward, 1866.

ALEXANDER, ROBERT L. "The Architecture of Russell Warren." Unpublished dissertation, New York University, 1952.
CRAM, RALPH ADAMS. *My Life in Architecture.* Boston: Little, Brown, 1936.
GARRIGAN, KRISTINE OTTESEN. *Ruskin On Architecture.* Madison: University of Wisconsin Press, 1973.
HAMLIN, TALBOT F. *Benjamin Henry Latrobe.* New York: Oxford University Press, 1955.
HITCHCOCK, HENRY-RUSSELL. "Ruskin and American Architecture, or Regeneration Long Delayed." From *Concerning Architecture,* ed. by John Summerson. London: Penguin, 1968.
John Holden Greene. Ed. by Mrs. Charles New. Providence, R.I.: Mowbray, 1972.
KERVICK, FRANCIS. *Architects in America of Catholic Tradition.* Rutland, Vt.: Tuttle, 1962.
KIMBALL, SIDNEY FISKE. *Thomas Jefferson, Architect.* Boston: Riverside Press, 1916.
KIRKER, HAROLD. *The Architecture of Charles Bulfinch.* Cambridge, Mass.: Harvard University Press, 1969.
LANDY, JACOB. *Minard Lafever.* New York: Columbia University Press, 1970.
NEWTON, ROGER HALE. *Town & Davis: Architects.* New York: Columbia University Press, 1942.
O'GORMAN, JAMES F. *The Architecture of Frank Furness.* Philadelphia: Philadelphia Museum of Art, 1973.
SCULLY, ARTHUR, JR. *James Dakin, Architect.* Baton Rouge: Louisiana State University Press, 1973.
STANTON, PHOEBE B. *Pugin.* New York: Viking, 1971.
UPJOHN, EVERARD MILLER. *Richard Upjohn, Architect and Churchman.* New York: Columbia University Press, 1939.

ADDISON, AGNES. *Romanticism and the Gothic Revival.* New York: Gordian Press, 1967.
AMORY, CLEVELAND. *The Last Resorts.* New York: Harper, 1952.
BURCHARD, JOHN, and ALBERT BUSH-BROWN. *The Architecture of America: A Social and Cultural History.* Boston: Little, Brown, 1961.
CLARK, KENNETH. *The Gothic Revival: An Essay in the History of Taste.* London: Murray, 1962. 3rd ed.
EARLY, JAMES. *Romanticism and American Architecture.* New York: A. S. Barnes, 1965.
GILLION, EDMUND V., JR. *Early Illustrations and Views of American Architecture.* New York: Dover Publications, 1971.
GOWANS, ALAN. *Images of American Living: Four Centuries of Architecture and Furniture as Cultural Expression.* Philadelphia: J. B. Lippincott, 1964.
HAMLIN, TALBOT F. *The American Spirit in Architecture.* New Haven: Yale University Press, 1926.
Historic American Buildings Survey Data Sheets. In the Collections of the Library of Congress, Division of Prints and Photographs; Historic American Buildings Survey; Commission of Fine Arts. An ongoing survey.
HITCHCOCK, HENRY-RUSSELL. *Architecture: Nineteenth and Twentieth Centuries.* Baltimore: Penguin, 1958.

III
BIOGRAPHIES
AND MONOGRAPHS

IV
HISTORIES, SURVEYS,
AND ANALYSES

LANCASTER, OSBERT. *Here, of all Places.* Boston: Houghton Mifflin, 1958.
LARKIN, OLIVER W. *Art and Life in America.* New York: Holt, Rinehart & Winston, 1964. Rev. ed.
LICHTEN, FRANCES. *Decorative Art of Victoria's Era.* New York: Scribner, 1950.
MAASS, JOHN. *The Gingerbread Age.* New York: Bramhall House, 1957.
———. *The Victorian Home in America.* New York: Hawthorne, 1972.
MORRISON, HUGH. *Early American Architecture.* New York: Oxford University Press, 1952.
National Register of Historic Places, Inventory-Nomination Forms. Prepared in the Offices of the State Historic Preservation Officers for Submission to the National Register, Office of Archeology and Historic Preservation, National Park Service, U. S. Department of the Interior. An ongoing survey.
SCHUYLER, MONTGOMERY. *American Architecture and Other Writings.* Ed. by William H. Jordy and Ralph Coe. Cambridge, Mass.: Harvard University Press, 1961.
SEALE, WILLIAM. *The Tasteful Interlude. American Interiors through the Camera's Eye 1860–1917.* New York: Praeger, 1975.
STANTON, PHOEBE B. *The Gothic Revival and American Church Architecture: An Episode in Taste 1840–1856.* Baltimore: Johns Hopkins Press, 1968.
WHIFFEN, MARCUS. *American Architecture Since 1780: A Guide to the Styles.* Cambridge, Mass.: M.I.T. Press, 1969.

V LOCAL AND REGIONAL STUDIES, ARCHITECTURAL GUIDEBOOKS

ANDREWS, WAYNE. *Architecture in Chicago and Mid-America.* New York: Atheneum, 1968.
———. *Architecture in Michigan.* Detroit: Wayne State University, 1967.
———. *Architecture in New York.* New York: Atheneum, 1969.
BERNHARDI, ROBERT. *The Buildings of Berkeley.* Berkeley, Calif.: Lederer, Street & Zeus, 1971.
BUNTING, BAINBRIDGE and ROBERT H. NYLANDER. *Survey of Architectural History in Cambridge. Report Four: Old Cambridge.* Cambridge, Mass.: M.I.T. Press, 1973.
CAMPEN, RICHARD N. *Architecture of The Western Reserve, 1800–1900.* Cleveland: Press of Case Western Reserve University, 1971.
CROCKER, MARY WALLACE. *Historic Architecture in Mississippi.* Jackson: University and College Press of Mississippi, 1973.
DALLAS, SANDRA. *Cherry Creek Gothic; Victorian Architecture in Denver.* Norman: University of Oklahoma Press, 1971.
DRURY, JOHN. *Historic Midwest Houses.* New York: Bonanza, 1947.
FERRY, W. HAWKINS. *The Buildings of Detroit.* Detroit: Wayne State University Press, 1971.
FOLSOM, MERRILL. *Great American Mansions.* New York: Hastings House, 1963.
GREIFF, CONSTANCE, MARY W. GIBBONS, and ELIZABETH G. C. MENZIES. *Princeton Architecture.* Princeton: Princeton University Press, 1967.
A Handbook of Information Concerning the Cathedral-Church of Bryn Athyn, Pennsylvania. Bryn Athyn: General Church Book Center, 1967. 9th ed.
HITCHCOCK, HENRY-RUSSELL. *Rhode Island Architecture.* Providence: Rhode Island Museum Press, 1939.
HOWELLS, JOHN MEAD. *The Architectural Heritage of the Merrimack.* New York: Architectural Book Publishing Co., 1941.
HOWLAND, RICHARD H. *The Architecture of Baltimore.* Baltimore: Johns Hopkins Press, 1953.
JACOBSEN, HUGH NEWELL. *A Guide to the Architecture of Washington, D.C.* New York: Praeger, 1965.
KELLY, JOHN FREDERICK. *Early Connecticut Meetinghouses.* New York: Columbia University Press, 1948.
KIRKER, HAROLD. *California's Architectural Frontier.* San Marino, Calif.: Huntington Library, 1960.

Koeper, Frederick. *Illinois Architecture From Territorial Times to the Present.* Chicago: University of Chicago Press, 1968.

Lancaster, Clay. *Ante Bellum Houses of the Bluegrass.* Lexington: University of Kentucky Press, 1961.

———. *The Architecture of Historic Nantucket.* New York: McGraw-Hill Book Co., 1972.

Linley, John. *Architecture of Middle Georgia.* Athens: University of Georgia Press, 1972.

Newcomb, Rexford. *Architecture of The Old North-West Territory.* Chicago: University of Chicago Press, 1950.

———. *Old Kentucky Architecture.* New York: W. Helburn, 1940.

New York Landmarks. Ed. by Allan Burnham. Middletown, Conn.: Wesleyan University Press, 1963.

Olmstead, Roger R. *Here Today: San Francisco's Architectural Heritage.* San Francisco: Chronicle Books, 1968.

O'Neal, William B. *Architecture in Virginia.* New York: Walker & Co., 1968.

Peat, Wilbur D. *Indiana Houses of the Nineteenth Century.* Indianapolis: Indiana Historical Society, 1962.

Philadelphia Architecture in the Nineteenth Century. Ed. by Theodore B. White. Philadelphia: University of Pennsylvania Press, 1953.

Ravenel, Beatrice St. Julien. *The Architects of Charleston.* Charleston: Carolina Art Association, 1946.

Rawlings, James Scott. *Virginia's Colonial Churches.* Richmond: Garrett & Massie, 1963.

Rettig, Robert Bell. *Guide to Cambridge Architecture: Ten Walking Tours.* Cambridge, Mass.: M.I.T. Press, 1969.

Scully, Vincent, and Antoinette Downing. *The Architectural Heritage of Newport, Rhode Island, 1640–1915.* Cambridge, Mass.: Harvard University Press, 1952.

Smith, R. A. *Smith's Illustrated Guide to and through Laurel Hill Cemetery.* Philadelphia: Willis P. Hazard, 1852.

Tarbell, Ida M. *Florida Architecture of Addison Mizner.* H. H. Smith, 1928.

Van Trump, James D., and Arthur P. Ziegler, Jr. *Landmark Architecture of Allegheny County, Pennsylvania.* Pittsburgh: Pittsburgh History & Landmarks Foundation, 1967.

Vaughan, Thomas, and George A. McMath. *A Century of Portland Architecture.* Portland: Oregon Historical Society, 1967.

Weaver, Glenn. *The History of Trinity College.* Vol. 1. Hartford: Trinity College Press, 1967.

VI PERIODICALS

Andrews, Wayne. "The Gothic Menace: Forerunner of Contemporary Architecture." *Historic Preservation* 22 (Jan.–March 1970).

"Concrete Blocks, Honolulu, 1870's." *JSAH* 11 (Oct. 1952).

Davidson, Ruth. "Roseland, A Gothic Revival Mansion." *Antiques* 81 (May 1962): 510–14.

Gaines, William H., Jr. "Bremo and Bremo Recess, A Home Dedicated to Service." *Virginia Cavalcade* 6 (Autumn 1956).

Landy, Jacob. "The Washington Monument Project in New York." *JSAH* 28 (Dec. 1969): 291–97.

Lang, S. "The Principles of the Gothic Revival in England." *JSAH* 25 (Dec. 1966).

Lyle, Royster, Jr., and Matthew W. Paxton, Jr. "The V.M.I. Barracks." *Virginia Cavalcade* 23 (Winter 1974).

Park, Helen. "A List of Architectural Books Available in America Before the Revolution." *JSAH* 20 (Oct. 1961).

Parsons, Kermit C. "The Quad on the Hill: An Account of the First Buildings at Cornell." *JSAH* 22 (Dec. 1963).

Patton, Glenn. "James Keys Wilson (1828–1894): Architect of the Gothic Revival in Cincinnati." *JSAH* 26 (Dec. 1969): 285–93.

Perusse, Lyle F. "The Gothic Revival in California." *JSAH* 14 (Oct. 1965).

Placzek, Adolf K. "Design for Columbia College, 1813." *JSAH* 11 (May 1952).

Rusk, Sarah E. "Hezekiah Eldridge, Architect–Builder of St. John's Church, Cleveland, Ohio." *JSAH* 25 (March 1966).

Salomon, Richard G. "Philander Chase, Norman Nash and Charles Bulfinch." *Historical Magazine of the Protestant Episcopal Church* 15 (1946).

Van Derpool, James Grote. "The Restoration of St. Luke's, Smithfield, Virginia." *JSAH* 17 (March 1958).

Wodehouse, Lawrence. "John Henry Hopkins and The Gothic Revival." *Antiques* 103 (April 1973).

VII
THE DECORATIVE ARTS

Bishop, Robert. *How to Know American Furniture.* New York: Dutton, 1973.

Butler, Joseph T. *American Furniture.* London: Tribune Books, 1973.

Downs, Joseph T. *American Furniture—Queen Anne and Chippendale Periods.* New York: Macmillan, 1952.

Hornor, William Macpherson, Jr. *Philadelphia Furniture.* Philadelphia: Privately Printed, 1935.

Lee, Ruth Webb. *Early American Pressed Glass.* Framingham Centre, Mass.: Privately Printed, 1933. 14th ed.

19th-Century America. Furniture and Other Decorative Arts. New York: Metropolitan Museum of Art, 1970.

Reif, Rita. *Treasure Rooms of America's Mansions, Manors, and Houses.* New York: Coward-McCann, 1970.

Sack, Albert. *Fine Points of Furniture.* New York: Crown, 1960.

Acknowledgments

It is with great pleasure that the authors take this opportunity to acknowledge the invaluable assistance extended to them by curators, librarians, archivists, and historians: William Beiswanger, Thomas Jefferson Memorial Foundation; Donald Burleson, Biltmore; William A. V. Cecil, Biltmore; S. Allen Chambers, Historic American Buildings Survey; Helen Chillman, Yale University; Virginia Daiker, Prints Division, Library of Congress; Mary Dunnington, Fiske Kimball Library, University of Virginia; Mrs. S. Henry Edmunds, Historic Charleston Foundation; James H. Goode, Smithsonian Institution; Linda Hewitt, Isabella Stewart Gardner Museum; Gregory A. Johnson, Alderman Library, University of Virginia; Charlotte LaRue, Museum of the City of New York; Robert F. Looney, Free Library of Philadelphia; Nancy Miller, Maryland

Historical Trust; Herbert Mitchell, Avery Architectural Library, Columbia University; Charles F. Montgomery, Mabel Brady Garvan Collection, Yale University; Dr. William Murtagh, Keeper of the National Register of Historic Places; William A. Oates, St. Paul's School; John F. Page, New Hampshire Historical Society; Adolf K. Placzek, Avery Architectural Library, Columbia University; Liza Reynolds, Mississippi Department of Archives and History; Charles B. Simmons, Henry Morrison Flagler Museum; Katherine M. Smith, Virginia State Library; Raymond Spencer, St. Paul's School; John A. H. Sweeney, Winterthur; and William Taggert, Lyndhurst.

Also, many thanks are due to persons who supplied research material or illustrations, among them: Mrs. Ruben Algood, Barbara Barlow, Lee Burtis, Bernard Carman, Earle Coleman, Mary Wallace Crocker, U. William Cunity, Dewey Lee Curtis, Jeffrey Darbee, Jo Dirkeson, Sandra Elder, Chris Finsness, Bruce Gill, Alvie Harding, Herbert L. Harper, Barbara Hunt, Robert E. Lee, Richard Lindquist, Gale Link, Al Louer, William T. Long, Bruce MacDougal, Elizabeth MacGregor, Paula Maxwell, Donald A. B. Mills, Joey Morgan, Kenneth Morrison, Roger W. Moss, Jr., Frank O'Brien, Mrs. Leonard Panaggio, Thomas Parker, Mrs. Arlene Peterson, Robert Reed, Thomas Rumner, Mrs. Francis Sanfort, Earle Shettleworth, Jr., Elizabeth Telford, E. H. Thomas, Earl W. Wolslagel, George Wrenn, III, and R. Eugene Zepp.

We are grateful to the owners of various houses, and others with buildings in their care, for their generous interest and cooperation: Mr. John Winthrop Aldrich, Mr. Lee B. Anderson, Mr. and Mrs. Lewis R. Andrews, Mr. and Mrs. Craig Bennett, James Biddle, Mr. Bennie Brown, Jr., Miss Alexandra Bruce, John A. Castellani, The Estate of S. P. Colt, Miss Sylvia Dakin, John W. Delafield, Jet Kellogg, Hayward F. Manice, Mrs. Edward Manigault, Mr. and Mrs. Frank Mauran, III, William L. Van Alen, and Mrs. McDonald Warner.

We are, in addition, much indebted to those acquaintances, friends, and colleagues who provided counsel, carried out research, and were lavish with their hospitality and assistance: Ford Ballard, Charles N. Bayless, Mr. and Mrs. Gilbert B. Benson, Marcus Binney, Mr. and Mrs. Thomas S. Brush, Mrs. Poe Burling, Richard Crowley, Robert C. Day, John W. Delafield, Mr. John Page Elliott, Jack L. Finglass, Mrs. Andrew A. Fraser, G. William Gahagan, Mark Gahagan, James Gibbons, James H. Grady, Wendy Grieder, Mrs. Iola S. Haverstick, Mrs. Nicholas Holmes, Miss Conover Hunt, W. Bradfield Hutchings, Richard H. Jenrette, Miss Olwen M. Jones, John B. Kirby, Jr., Mr. and Mrs. George Kopperl, Mills Lane, IV, Floyd Logan, Royster Lyle, Jr., Mrs. Florene Maine, Mrs. William R. Miller, William Morgan, Mrs. Sydney H. Moore, Dr. Charles Peterson, David Pettigrew, William Pillsbury, Mrs. John H. Sadler, Miss Sue Ann Sadler, William Seale, Dr. Clement M. Silvestro, Dr. Phoebe B. Stanton, Walter Knight Sturges, Edward Swain, III, Mr. and Mrs. Douglas Thoms, Douglass Shand Tucci, Dell T. Upton, Mr. and Mrs. Clark van der Lyke, Lady Betty Webster, Roy H. Wolvin, Jr., and John G. Zehmer.

We wish to express particular appreciation to John MacLellan, Richard Keppleman, Mary Kilduff, and the entire staff of the Virginia Historic Landmarks Commission for their patience and encouragement. Finally, we offer most heartfelt thanks to Irene Evangelisti for her swift and meticulous typing, and to Donald Ackland, Betsy Beach, and Robin Bledsoe of the New York Graphic Society, who have spared no pains in the production of the book, while preserving a heartening attitude of serene good cheer.

Index

Illustration pages are indicated in italic type; text often also appears on these pages.

Photograph Credits

The illustrations are reproduced by the courtesy of the following sources. Art Institute of Chicago: 104 right; Association for the Preservation of Tennessee Antiquities: 52 right; Athenaeum of Philadelphia: 32; Avery Architectural Library, Columbia University: 40, 45, 56, 59, 157 right; Pietro Belluschi: 168 top left; Bancroft Library, University of California, Berkeley: 145 left; William L. Beiswanger: 22 lower left; Boston Athenaeum (photo George M. Cushing, from *The History and Antiquities of the See & Cathedral Church of Norwich*, 1816), 1; Bostonian Society: 34 left; Boston Public Library: 117 left; California State Library: 101; Carolina Art Association: 64; Carpenters' Company of the City and County of Philadelphia: 18; Cathedral Church of Bryn Athyn: 152; Cathedral Church of St. John the Divine: 151 right; William A. V. Cecil: 144; Samuel Chamberlain: 21; Richard Cheek: 36 right; Chicago Historical Society: 131 (photo Norman A. Tegtmeyer), 165 left and right; Connecticut State Library: 146 lower left; Mary Wallace Crocker: 62 right, 79 bottom, 110 top; Miss Sylvia Dakin: 100 bottom; Dossin Great Lakes Museum: 146 top left and right; John Page Elliott: 73 left; Family Lines System: 83 top; Free Library of Philadelphia: 23, 130; Harvard University Archives: 55 left, 117 right; Paul H. Henning, Infinite Eye Studio: 121 (stitchery by National Paragon Corp.); Tucker Herrin Hill: 106 top left; Historical Society of Pennsylvania: 29; Historic American Buildings Survey, Library of Congress: 10, 24 right, 33 left, 81 right, 102 left, 125 right, 132 lower right; Jack Boucher for HABS: 51 top, 77, 88 right, 128, 129, 131 right; Theodore F. Dillon for HABS: 102 right; Louis I. Schwartz for HABS: 22 top; John T. Hopf: 143 right; Indiana Historical Society: 81 left; Inter-American Defense Board: 120 right; Kenyon College: 41; Knox College: 91; Library Company of Philadelphia: 16 right; Library of Congress: 9 right, 20 right, 31 left, 34 right, 44, 70 bottom, 132 lower left, 147; Frances Benjamin Johnston Collection, Library of Congress: 14 lower right, 26 bottom, 27, 79 top, 162; Arnold Rothstein for Farm Security Administration, Library of Congress: 124; Litchfield Historical Society: 123 left; Calder Loth: 6, 14 lower left, 25 right, 33 right, 37, 38, 51 lower right, 60 right, 78 top, 89 left, 93 left and center, 107, 115 lower left, 120 left, 123 right, 131 left, 153, 159; Louisiana State Museum: 86; Louisiana Tourist Development Commission: 141 right; Marine Historical Association, Inc., Mystic Seaport, 54, 170 top; Howard Marler: 25 left; Maryland National Capital Park and Planning Commission: 17 bottom (photo Kathryn Sentelle); Massachusetts Historical Society: 22 lower right; Metropolitan Museum of Art: 46, 49, 73 right, 74; Mountain Lake Sanctuary: 161; Museum of Fine Arts, Boston: 92; Museum of the City of New York: 60 left, 63, 115 top; National Trust for Historic Preservation: 145 right, 171; New-York Historical Society: 48 left, 85; New York State Commerce Department: 158; New York State Historical Association: 43; North Carolina State Department of Archives and History: 62 left; Northwestern National Life Insurance Company: 168 bottom; Ohio Historical Society: 140; Oregon Historical Society: 89 right, 132 top; Oregon State Highway Division: 98 right; Peale Museum: 50; Pennsylvania Academy of the Fine Arts: 116; Pennsylvania Historical Society: 163; Preservation Society of Newport County: 143 left (photo John T. Hopf); Princeton University Archives: 90 top, 119, 151 left; Reorganized Church of Jesus Christ of Latter-Day Saints: 51 lower left; Ringling Museum: 160 bottom; Royal Academy of Arts: 112; St. Paul's School: 126; St. Thomas' Church: 149; J. Sadler: 24 left, 53 right, 55 right, 76, 80, 82, 88 left, 93 right, 103 bottom, 109 left, 110 lower left, 111 left, 115 lower right, 134, 137, 139, 141 left, 142, 154, 160 upper right, 165 center, 167, 170 bottom; J. Sadler Collection: 9 left, 19, 39, 75, 94, 95, 109 right, 137, 160 top; Smithsonian Institution: 30, 68, 69, 70 top, 83 bottom; K. M. Starkweather: 104 left; Edward Swain, III: 109 bottom; Carol Teller: 72 right; Trinity College: 138 left; Union College: 118; United States Air Force Academy: 168 upper right; University of Pittsburgh: 166; University of Virginia, Alderman Library: 35, 84 (from *Smith's Illustrated Guide to and through Laurel Hill Cemetery*), 138; University of Virginia, Fiske Kimball Library: 87, 97 top, 108, 111 right; Utah State Historical Society: 125 left; Virginia Historic Landmarks Commission: 71 (photo Katherine T. Read); Virginia Museum of Fine Arts: 31 right, 78 bottom, 135; Virginia State Library: 3, 7 (courtesy Association for the Preservation of Virginia Antiquities), 8, 11, 13, 14 top, 17 top, 20 left, 26 top, 28, 36 left, 42, 48 right, 52 left, 57, 65, 67, 72 left, 90 lower left and right, 96, 97 bottom, 98 left, 100 top, 105, 106 top right and bottom, 110 lower left, 127, 133, 136; Washington Cathedral: 156, 157 left (photo Robert C. Lautman), 169; Washington University: 155 (photo Herb Weitman); Women's Christian Temperance Union: 103 top; Yale University Art Gallery: vi , 16 left.